AMERICAN HERITAGE
ILLUSTRATED HISTORY
OF THE UNITED STATES

The battle of Palo Alto, fought on May 8, 1846, was part of the Mexican War. The officer on the left on the white horse is probably Zachary Taylor.
LIBRARY OF CONGRESS

FRONT COVER: *Detail of the 1848 Nathaniel Currier Lithograph* The Attack on the Castle of Chapultepec.
LIBRARY OF CONGRESS

FRONT ENDSHEET: *Marching to Mexico City, the American forces attack the fortified convent at Churubusco in one of the battles in the Mexican War.*
OFFICE OF THE CHIEF OF MILITARY HISTORY, U.S. ARMY

CONTENTS PAGE: *The North's excited response to Lincoln's April, 1861 call for 75,000 military volunteers is expressed in this print, titled* The Spirit of '61.
COLLECTION OF MRS. KATHARINE COOK KNOX

BACK ENDSHEET: *The Confederate flag at Fort Sumter, which was not hauled down until February, 1865, was a proud and defiant symbol of the South's cause.*
CONFEDERATE MUSEUM

BACK COVER: *This 1848 Nathaniel Currier lithograph (top)* The Attack on the Castle of Chapultepec *shows American troops advancing in this important victory in the Mexican War; by the 1850s the institution of slavery, as depicted in this romanticized plantation scene (bottom left), had polarized America; the militant abolitionist John Brown (bottom right) seized the federal arsenal at Harper's Ferry, Virginia, in 1859.*
LIBRARY OF CONGRESS; METROPOLITAN MUSEUM OF ART; LIBRARY OF CONGRESS

AMERICAN HERITAGE
ILLUSTRATED HISTORY
OF THE UNITED STATES

VOLUME 7

WAR WITH MEXICO

BY ROBERT G. ATHEARN

Created in Association with the
Editors of AMERICAN HERITAGE

and for the updated edition
MEDIA PROJECTS INCORPORATED

CHOICE PUBLISHING, INC.
New York

Library of Congress Catalog Card Number: 87–73399
ISBN 0–945260–07–5
ISBN 0-945260-00-8

This 1988 edition is published and distributed by Choice Publishing, Inc., 53 Watermill Lane, Great Neck, NY 11021 by arrangement with American Heritage, a division of Forbes, Inc.

Manufactured in the United States of America
10 9 8 7 6 5 4

CONTENTS OF THE COMPLETE SERIES

Editor's Note to the Revised Edition
Introduction by ALLAN NEVINS
Main text by ROBERT G. ATHEARN

EACH VOLUME CONTAINS AN ENCYCLOPEDIC SECTION; MASTER INDEX IN VOLUME 18

GOD. OUR COUNTRY AND LIBERTY.!!

THE SPIRIT OF '61.

Up with the Standard and bear it on ! Remember the deeds of Washington.
Let its folds to the wind expand ; And the flag of our native land.

CONTENTS OF VOLUME 7

544

CHAPTER 19

THE CURTAIN RAISER

Although the Mexican War is not highly regarded by many Americans, and is certainly far overshadowed by the Civil War as a turning point in American history, nevertheless it played a significant role as a divider between early and later phases of the nation's development. It brought to a climax the continental expansion of the preceding quarter-century; it severely aggravated the American sectional issue and brought its differences into much sharper focus; and it contributed heavily to the political commotion of the 1850s.

For nearly 20 years, the Mexican government had been under mounting pressure from the United States to sell Texas, California, or practically any other part of the Southwest. With each refusal, friction between the two countries increased, and the situation finally came to a head over Texas. Mexico had been annoyed by the American volunteers who poured into Texas to aid in the revolution, and

The Mexican War was the big topic of its day, and when the newspaper arrived in town with news of it, the citizens eagerly gathered to hear reports of the battles.

after the United States invited Texas to join the Union in March, 1845, Mexico broke off diplomatic relations. President James K. Polk countered by sending troops under General Zachary Taylor to Corpus Christi on the Texas coast. Then, in the fall of 1845, the United States again made a monetary offer, this time for Upper California and New Mexico and for a section of land between the Nueces River and the Rio Grande. But the Mexican government refused to listen to John Slidell, the American emissary who came to make the proposal.

After the failure of Slidell's mission, Taylor occupied Point Isabel, at the mouth of the Rio Grande, in March, 1846. Despite a warning from the Mexicans that his action constituted aggression, Taylor refused to budge, and blockaded the river, sealing off the Mexican city of Matamoros from ocean traffic.

From the Mexican viewpoint, this was not the first time the Americans had thrown down the gauntlet. In 1836, when the Texas revolution was in full swing, General Edmund Gaines had ordered American troops to chase Indian raiders out of the United States

James K. Polk

and into strife-torn Texas. This entrance into what the Mexicans considered their territory (and they had a point, as the Texans had not yet proved they could hold the land they declared free) irritated officials at Mexico City, who sent vigorous complaints to Washington. American interest in Texas was well known, and the presence of United States troops in that territory during the rebellion was anything but reassuring to the Mexican government.

In 1842, in California, an event had occurred that—once it was stripped of its comic-opera aspects—could be taken by the Mexicans as evidence of their northern neighbor's aggressive intentions. That autumn, Commodore Thomas ap Catesby Jones, who was at the time in Peru, received a rumor that hostilities between the United States and Mexico had begun. Not waiting for further confirmation, he headed for California, determined to do his part in defending American interests. At Monterey the commodore sent ashore a contingent of men, who announced their mission to the amazed residents of that sleepy outpost and then ran up the American flag. The next day, the triumphant Jones made the mortifying discovery that there was no war—a revelation that called for the most profuse apologies, salutes to the Mexican ensign, and a hasty lowering of the American flag. The Mexican governor responded with an elaborate ball, and amidst the warmest evidences of California hospitality, the embarrassed guests withdrew.

Of all the provocations Mexico felt it had received, the American annexation of Texas, followed by claims that the Rio Grande was the correct southern boundary of the new state, was the worst. Taylor's march across the disputed area and his blockade of the river were regarded by Mexico as an act of war. That government had not regarded the Rio Grande as a boundary of Texas prior to Texan independence; why should it do so now?

In Washington, President Polk was considering recommending a declaration of war to Congress on the grounds that Mexico had not paid its American debts, that it would not receive an emissary to discuss differences, and that it appeared disinclined to settle various disputes by peaceful means. Just before preparing such a message, he was afforded what he considered a more valid reason for taking up arms. Early in May, 1846, the President learned that some two weeks earlier a Mexican force had crossed the Rio Grande and had encountered an American patrol. In the fray that followed, 16 Americans were killed or wounded and the rest captured. In Washington it was immediately assumed that American troops had been killed upon American soil (a premise the Mexicans could argue because they also claimed the land) and that war was the inevitable consequence. Polk presented this view to Congress when he announced that Mexicans had crossed the boundary, invaded the United States, and "shed American blood upon American soil." The legislators agreed with Polk and promptly appropriated $10,000,000 for the support of 50,000 volunteers.

With the opening formalities concluded, Polk now instructed General Taylor to get on with the war and con-

The Mexican governor gave Commodore Jones a party, similar to the one above, in the Spanish aristocratic tradition, after his false conquest of Monterey.

General Winfield Scott reviewed his troops after he had marched them trium-phantly into Mexico City on September 14, 1847, at the end of the Mexican War.

quer the enemy. By September, Taylor had pushed the Mexicans back from the Rio Grande and was in possession of the city of Monterrey, but instead of being pleased, such progress seemed to worry Polk. Taylor had become a national hero, and the Whigs were beginning to talk about the general as a Presidential prospect. Polk, a Democrat, had no fully qualified Democratic general at his disposal, so he finally decided to appoint Winfield Scott, another Whig general, but one less likely to aspire to high office, to command an expeditionary force that was to be sent to Veracruz and on to Mexico City. Meanwhile, another group, the Army of the West, marched from the Missouri River to Santa Fe. Colonel (later General) Stephen W. Kearny took parts of it on to California while Colonel A. W. Doniphan and 300 volunteers went south to capture the city of Chihuahua.

In Mexico, nearly half of Taylor's men were detached to join Scott, but even so, Taylor succeeded in driving off a superior Mexican force at the Battle of Buena Vista in February, 1847. A month later, the final campaign of the war began with the landing of United States troops at Veracruz. By the end of March, 1847, the trek from the sea to the Mexican capital was under way. Hard fighting marked the route, but by August, Scott's army was before Mexico City. There was a brief respite while preliminary peace talks were held, but they failed and Scott resumed his attack. The Americans finally entered the city in mid-September, and a few months later, on February 2, 1848, the Treaty of Guadalupe Hidalgo was concluded.

The agreement confirmed American claims to the Rio Grande as a boundary and awarded to the United States the vast Southwest, including the present states of California, Nevada, and Utah, with parts of Arizona, New Mexico, Colorado, and Wyoming. This huge empire, with Texas, added nearly 2,000,000 square miles to the nation. By the terms of the treaty, claims of American citizens against the Mexican government were assumed by the United States and a general pacifier of $15,000,000 was given to the defeated side. Although Polk was not happy with the treaty, he was so fearful of what the more unreasonable elements among American expansionists might propose as a substitute that he agreed to accept the document of February 2. Except for the Gadsden Purchase of 1853, the American continental boundaries were now complete.

War-born sectionalism

The Mexican War provided far more problems than it solved—among them a sharpening of the sectional issue. Clement Eaton in his *History of the Old South* stated flatly, "One of the most important consequences of the Mexican War was that it precipitated a great sectional struggle between the North and the South over the status of slavery in this territory, a controversy that eventually led to the Civil War." He held that the conflict was "an adventure in imperialism of the South in partnership with the restless inhabitants of the West"—a conflict that was "provoked by a Southern President and fought largely by Southern generals and by Southern volunteers."

The event that securely linked the Mexican War to sectional rivalry was precipitated by an obscure Democratic Congressman from Pennsylvania named David Wilmot. In the late summer of 1846, long before the American people were faced by the problem of what to do with lands gained at the Treaty of Guadalupe Hidalgo, Polk's administration had asked for $2,000,000 to buy additional territory from Mexico. Wilmot, searching for a means of gaining political support from his constituents, seized upon the opportunity to attach a rider forever barring the institution of slavery from any lands gained from Mexico. While such a notion might appeal to Wilmot's antislavery friends at home, it contained enough political dynamite to send reverberations clear across the land. Southerners—both Whigs and Democrats—loudly denounced the move, while Northern Free Soilers, growing daily more vociferous, praised it. Although the Wilmot Proviso was never adopted by Congress, it became the guiding principle of moderate antislavery men—men who would leave slavery alone in states where it existed but who were determined to prevent its spread into new territories.

News from Mexico tended to obscure the Southern outrage occasioned by Wilmot's proposal. For a brief moment, sectionalism was eclipsed by a flurry of resurgent nationalism. But those who hoped to preserve the bonds of union could not always expect such coincidental occurrences. One day, appeals to nationalistic pride would not be enough to keep the two great American sections from meeting each other in combat.

The Mexican War's conclusion was followed by the election of a military hero to high office, an event that already was becoming an American tradition. Despite Polk's attempts to bury him politically, Zachary Taylor emerged a war hero and ran for the Presidency on the Whig ticket. The Democrats nominated Lewis Cass of Michigan, while a group of political dissidents chose Martin Van Buren as the candidate of the Free Soil Party. The latter group was the only one to take a stand on the slave issue, with a platform of "Free soil, free speech, free labor, and free men." This appeal to those who wanted free homesteads and to those who harbored antislave sentiments did not put Van Buren into the White House again, but his appearance in the campaign siphoned off enough Democratic votes to defeat Cass and elect Taylor.

Although the presence of the Free Soilers in the campaign signified the

During the gold rush, long lines formed outside the post office in San Francisco for the monthly delivery of all mail to miners in northern California.

rising importance of the slavery question, no one seemed to know how the man who won the election felt about that subject. Taylor, a slaveholder from Louisiana, might have been expected to favor the Southern view, but his opinions on the issue were not clear even after his election. Yet now that the Mexican conflict was over, the questions raised by the Wilmot Proviso were bound to reappear.

The newly conquered territory stood waiting for a settlement of its political future. The fact that Taylor and his party were committed to nothing politically gave them only a brief respite at best. Sooner or later some kind of solution had to be found.

The urgent necessity for a decision was brought home to the President and Congress by the news from newly won California. In 1848, gold was discovered at John Sutter's mill on the American River, setting off one of the greatest population movements in history. The forty-niners and those who followed them poured westward in such numbers that some government organization was essential. During the fall of 1849, the Californians wrote an antislave constitution and organized a government, and early in 1850 applied for admission to the Union. The situation might not have been so difficult under other circumstances, but California was opening

On January 28, 1850, the 72-year-old Henry Clay presented the Compromise of 1850. Calhoun stands second from the right. Webster is seated, hand to head.

up the whole slavery question again. From the time of Missouri's admission, slave and free states had been taken into the Union in pairs to maintain the balance in Congress. Now that balance was threatened. There was no slave state to be matched with California, and Southern supporters were in no mood to welcome into their midst two new antislavery Senators.

Despite strong sectional loyalties, there was an underlying desire for a settlement that would prevent a serious conflict among Americans. President Taylor strongly urged compromise, suggesting that California be admitted as a free state and that the remainder of the Southwest be organized into territories without any reference to slavery. John C. Calhoun and his followers loudly denounced this idea, saying that the South had endured wrongs and insults from the North long enough, and there would be no more yielding, even if disunion was the price of standing firm.

The Senate heard a proposal by the Great Compromiser, Henry Clay, who suggested that California be admitted as a free state without any reference to slavery, and that the territory recently wrested from Mexico

552

be granted territorial government with no mention of the "peculiar institution." So far, this was Taylor's plan. In addition, Clay suggested that the slave trade—but not slavery—be abolished in the District of Columbia. To give the Southerners something, he recommended the enactment of a strong fugitive-slave law, one that would guarantee slaveowners the return of their escaped bondsmen. As further reassurance to them, Congress was to go on record with a statement that it had no control over the domestic slave trade. Finally, he proposed that the argument over Texas' western boundary be resolved by shortening it somewhat and in return compensating Texas by the federal assumption of her debts.

The 72-year-old Clay was dying, and this was the last of his great compromise suggestions, but it generated a series of debates in the Senate that were of historic import. All during the spring of 1850, the talk went on, with such towering figures as Calhoun, Clay, and Daniel Webster taking part. To their voices was added that of a new political power, one day to be called the Republican Party, now represented in the person of Senator William H. Seward of New York.

On the 4th of March, 1850, Calhoun, old and too weak to speak, was carried into the Senate and the packed galleries heard a friend read the old warrior's speech. He would die in less than a month, but now he was making his final plea for the South, rejecting

William H. Seward

the idea of compromise, insisting that the wrongs done his section be righted. Three days later the "godlike Daniel" Webster rose to deliver his historic 7th of March speech. His eloquence in behalf of union and moderation went down in the record as one of his last great efforts. Supporting Clay's plan all the way, Webster underscored the extreme nature of Calhoun's approach, and his words made a deep impression upon his colleagues.

Seward spoke on March 11 to a chamber that was nearly empty. Opposing compromise, predicting the natural downfall of the institution of slavery, he condemned Calhoun's suggestion that there be inserted into the Constitution a provision that would "restore to the South in substance the power she possessed," holding that it would afford that region an unequal advantage. Should that come to pass, he said, there was a "higher law" than the Constitution "which regulates our authority over the domain." His vague references to a higher law enraged Southern listeners but appealed to Free Soil elements in the North, who adopted the phrase as a slogan in the coming decade.

At the height of the impasse, fate stepped in to alter the situation. President Zachary Taylor died suddenly on July 9, 1850. His successor, Millard Fillmore, had antislavery sentiments, but he also harbored a burning hatred for Seward, which meant he would probably avoid the latter's extremism. When the new President appointed a cabinet favoring compromise, with Webster as Secretary of State, he demonstrated his administration's desire for moderation. Shortly the jigsaw-puzzle parts of settlement began to fall into place. During August and September, laws were passed to provide in general for Clay's suggestions, and when they were signed into law, the Compromise of 1850 was complete.

Peace, prosperity—and problems

For many reasons the Compromise of 1850 was welcomed by the American people. It seemed to promise "peace in our time"—to use a phrase of the 20th century—and a quieting of the persistent sectionalism question.

New problems arising out of the Mexican War and old ones aggravated by it apparently were set at rest. The discovery of gold in California had come in 1848, about the time of the Treaty of Guadalupe Hidalgo, and by the following year the forty-niners were making history on the Pacific Coast. Gold pouring through the arteries of the American economy brought an inflationary boom. Farm prices rose, commerce flourished, and businessmen glowed with optimism. So did plantation owners, whose cotton prices benefited from the improved situation. Moderates, North *and* South, urged an end to agitation.

The popularity of the Compromise was borne out by the election of 1852, in which the Democrat Franklin Pierce, who wholeheartedly endorsed the Compromise, was elected to the Presidency over the Whig candidate, General Winfield Scott, and the Free Soil nominee, John P. Hale. For a brief time, the fires of sectional strife appeared to have been extinguished, but resentments still smoldered deep under the surface. Abolitionist propaganda, so offensive to Southern slaveholders, continued to flow out of the North, particularly New England. To make matters worse, some Northerners showed little disposition to obey the fugitive-slave provision of the Compromise of 1850. Abolitionists gleefully participated in the "underground railroad," an organized means of smuggling slaves northward to Canada and freedom. Others openly

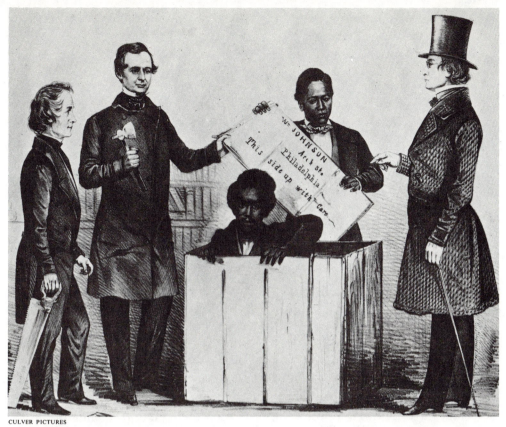

Henry Brown, a Southern slave, is placed by friends in a box labeled "This side up with care," to be shipped via express to Philadelphia and to freedom.

defied law officers by using physical force to prevent slaves from being returned to their owners. All this kept the slave question sharply before the American public, and the appearance of Harriet Beecher Stowe's inflammatory book, *Uncle Tom's Cabin,* fired the already excited passions in North and South alike.

Then in 1854 the old sectional controversy was reopened when Senator Stephen A. Douglas, of Illinois, introduced a Congressional measure to organize the territories of Kansas and Nebraska. Douglas' proposal included two special provisions that outraged Northern moderates as well as anti-slavery elements. The first was an idea

that Douglas called "popular sovereignty," which would allow the people of a territory to decide for themselves whether or not to permit slavery when the time for statehood came. The other provision would repeal the Missouri Compromise. The act could open the way to the spread of the slave system in all territories.

Probably Douglas was more interested in organizing Kansas and Nebraska for the purpose of obtaining a northern route for a transcontinental railroad than he was in furthering the spread of slavery. But in the outcry and clamor over his proposal, this fact was lost. To Northerners, and especially to abolitionists, it looked like a

After the Kansas-Nebraska Act was passed in 1854, bands of men known as Border Ruffians came from Missouri into Kansas to create a new slave state.

deep-laid slave plot. They were convinced of it when Jefferson Davis agreed to give up, in return for acceptance of popular sovereignty, his pet project of a southern route for the transcontinental railroad. Undisturbed by strong Northern protests, Davis, the Secretary of War, prevailed upon President Pierce to back the Kansas-Nebraska bill. The administration made it clear that patronage would be withheld from Democrats who opposed the measure, and it became law in May, 1854.

The Kansas-Nebraska Act is significant for what it symbolized. Up to the time of its passage, abolitionists had fought the institution of slavery, attempting to stamp it out. Yet only a few Americans wanted to go that far. Then, when it appeared that slavery might jump its bounds and spread beyond the containment line of 36°30′, many people became alarmed. Even to those who had no strong feelings in the matter, the move seemed to climax a long period of Southern aggressions. If slavery were permitted to spread into Kansas and Nebraska, it was feared that nonslave settlement would be hindered. Opponents of the act assumed that if slavery could expand, it would. In reality, topography and climatic conditions discouraged the extension of the system.

In 1854, soon after the passage of the territorial act, the government opened a land office in Kansas, despite the fact that Indian land titles were still in effect. At once the rush was on. Many farmers moved in from Iowa, Indiana, and Illinois. New Englanders, many of them backed financially by various "emigrant-aid societies," came to plant antislave sentiments along with crops. Southerners arrived in even greater numbers, and that fall they carried the local elections. The first Kansas territorial legislature, controlled by proslave elements, quickly drafted legislation to protect their "peculiar institution."

Northern fears appeared to have been realized; highly alarmed, they redoubled their efforts to populate Kansas with freemen. Many of the newcomers carried Sharps rifles, which they called Beecher's Bibles in reference to abolitionist clergyman Henry Ward Beecher, who had said there might be occasions when a gun was more useful than a Bible.

By 1855, Kansas was in turmoil, with constant outbreaks of violence between proslave and antislave forces. Soon each side had its own elected government, which it claimed as the lawful one, and by 1856 civil war had broken out. In May, a group of Southern Border Ruffians rode into the free-state town of Lawrence and destroyed it. A fanatic abolitionist named John Brown promptly struck back, murdering five proslavery settlers near Pottawatomie Creek. Both sides rushed to arms, giving rise to the term Bleeding Kansas. The first phase of the Civil War was on.

The politics of sectionalism

Not only in Kansas was this militant spirit evident. From the time of the Wilmot Proviso, antislavery Northerners had joined together politically

John Brown

in opposition to the expansion of the "slavocracy." In 1854, under the awkward phrase Anti-Nebraska, they voiced increasingly loud objections to Southern moves. At a mass meeting held at Jackson, Michigan, in July of that year, they adopted the name Republican. This new party, made up of abolitionists, old-line Whigs, Free Soilers, and antislavery Democrats, demanded the repeal of the Kansas-Nebraska Act and the fugitive-slave law, and advocated the abolition of slavery in the District of Columbia.

In 1856, the Republicans boldly entered the national political contest, determined to take over the reins of government. They had good reason to be optimistic. The Democratic Party was badly split, and the old Whig Party had fallen apart in the fight over the Kansas-Nebraska Act. The young

James Buchanan

SOUTHERN CHIVALR

Abolitionist Charles Sumner was caned in the

Republican organization nominated John C. Fremont, son-in-law of Missouri's Thomas Hart Benton. It denounced the repeal of the Missouri Compromise, attacked Southern expansionism, and pledged itself to destroy those "twin relics of barbarism" —slavery and polygamy.

Even though the total popular vote of the non-Democratic parties exceeded theirs, the Democrats managed to get control of both houses of Congress, and their Presidential candidate, James Buchanan, won by a narrow margin. The voting had revealed two significant developments: The election was along sectional lines, with Buchanan carrying the entire South, and the new Republican Party had proved surprisingly strong. This meant that the contest of 1860 would probably be decided on sectional issues, between Democrats and Republicans. And there was little promise of political peace during Buchanan's time in office.

In the 1856 campaign, the intensity of sectional feeling had been plain. That spring, Senator Charles Sumner of Massachusetts delivered to his colleagues a violent anti-Southern speech called *The Crime Against Kansas*. In it he bitterly denounced Senator A. P. Butler of South Carolina, who was absent. The assault was too much for Southern pride. Preston Brooks, a member of Congress and a relative of Butler's, entered the Senate after the debate and beat Sumner into insensibility with his cane. The victim did not attend Congressional sessions again for three years. Brooks was hailed as a hero in the South and was presented with a number of new canes as a tribute to his action. Naturally, North-

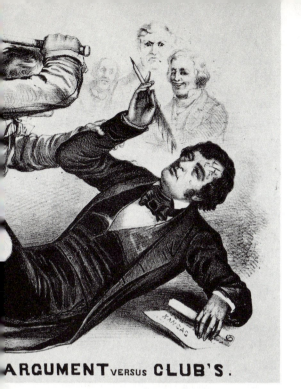

ARGUMENT versus CLUB'S.

Senate by Preston Brooks for his views on Kansas.

Dred Scott

erners seethed over Brooks' attack.

Hard on the heels of Bleeding Kansas and Bleeding Sumner came another disturbing event. Shortly after Buchanan's inauguration in the spring of 1857, the Supreme Court handed down the Dred Scott decision, and the uproar over slavery increased.

Dred Scott was a Missouri slave who had been taken north by his master. After returning to Missouri the master died, and the Negro sued for his freedom on the grounds that he had resided in a free state and was therefore a freeman. Although a Missouri court decided against him, Scott appealed, and the case finally reached the Supreme Court. A decision in Scott's favor would have meant widespread repercussions, because other Negroes in the same situation would be able to sue for their freedom. If no slaveowner dared to take his "property" into a free state, this would further curb the "peculiar institution."

But the decision went against Scott, on three counts: (1) As a slave, he was not a citizen of the United States and was not entitled to sue in the federal courts. (2) He was a resident of Missouri, so Illinois (the free state where he had lived) had no jurisdiction over him. (3) He could not be freed as a result of living north of the 36° 30′ line established by the Missouri Compromise, because Congress had no right to deprive citizens of their property (slaves) without due process of law.

The high court's ruling caused a considerable stir. The decision meant that the Missouri Compromise of 1820 was void, because any Southern resident could take his property north of 36° 30′ and have it protected by federal law. The case also delivered a severe blow to the concept of popular sovereignty. Under Douglas' theory, residents of the territories were to have a choice for or against slavery, but this decision voided it. If residents of a territory prohibited slavery, they would be depriving slaveholders of their private property without due process of law.

Political crisis

By the time the voters went to the polls for the mid-term election in 1858, the rift between North and South was more apparent than at any previous time. The Democratic Party was breaking up over sectionalism, and the Republicans, encouraged by their showing two years earlier, were stepping up their attacks. The financial panic of 1857 had shaken the business world, and Republicans were blaming hard times on the Democratic low tariff. The new party now had two weapons—antislavery and the tariff. Both issues tended to split the Democrats even further.

The most spectacular political contest of 1858 was the one for Senator from Illinois. It was between Democratic Senator Douglas, trying desperately to save his office in the face of mounting criticism against his party, and his Republican opponent, Abraham Lincoln. In a series of widely publicized debates, the "Little Giant" argued the major issues of the day with the tall, angular "Rail Splitter." At the beginning of this campaign, on June 16, 1858, Lincoln made his *House Divided* speech. "I believe this government cannot endure permanently half slave and half free," he told his listeners. "I do not expect the Union to be dissolved; I do not expect the house to fall; but I do expect it will cease to be divided. It will become all one thing, or all the other." He stated his belief that either the spread of slavery would be halted or that it would become lawful in all states, North as well as South.

In one of the debates between the two men, held at Freeport, Illinois, in August, Lincoln asked his opponent if the voters could, by popular sovereignty, keep slavery out of the territories. If Douglas said no, he would deny his own principle of popular sovereignty. If he said yes, he would go against the Dred Scott decision and draw the fire of Southern leaders. The Little Giant replied that, no matter what the Supreme Court said, the people of a territory had the power to accept or reject the institution of slavery. This statement of opinion became known as the Freeport Doctrine, and it helped Douglas retain his Senate seat. But he paid a price for it. By winning this battle, he lost the war, for his campaign statements were not well received in the South. Once widely popular there, he now fell into disfavor and lost the political strength that he would need in 1860. His moves also helped to split the Northern and Southern Democrats, further widening the gap between North and South.

LIBRARY OF CONGRESS

WAR IN THE WEST

Although the Mexican War began officially on May 13, 1846, and ended with the United States and a defeated Mexico signing a peace treaty in 1848, it had really begun in 1836. At that time, the American settlers in Mexican-held Texas declared their independence. They fought off the Mexican troops that came to subdue them, and in less than two months, they had won their freedom and become an independent republic. For the next nine years, the Texans and Mexicans quarreled; sometimes the quarrels became armed clashes. In March, 1845, the United States decided to annex Texas, despite Mexican protests. This act furthered the friction that already existed, and finally, in May, 1846, the United States declared war. When, in June, the American settlers in California demanded their independence from Mexico, it became apparent that the United States might also win a Pacific empire. After 16 months of fighting, the Americans defeated Mexico, and the vanquished nation was stripped of two-fifths of her territory. Texas was already gone; now California and New Mexico became part of the United States.

561

WAR IN THE WEST

THE DEFEAT AT THE ALAMO

Davy Crockett (center), lifting his famous rifle Betsy, tries to beat off the Mexican troops outside the Alamo on March 6, 1836. He was one of the 187 men who held the fortified San Antonio mission for 11 days against Santa Anna's army of 3,000, but finally he and all the other defenders were dead. The painting is by the 19th-century Texan, Robert Onderdonk.

LONE STAR

On March 2, 1836, during the siege of the Alamo, Texas declared its independence from Mexico, adopting the Lone Star flag at the right as its national banner. But independence did not become a reality for the Texans until they defeated Santa Anna's army at San Jacinto on April 21. General Sam Houston, wounded in battle, lies on a blanket as he accepts the surrender of Santa Anna, dressed in green tunic and white breeches. Deaf Smith (right), the Western scout, cups his ear to hear the terms. Painting by William H. Huddle.

THE WAR BEGINS

On May 13, 1846, President of the United States James Polk signed a bill declaring war on Mexico. His action did not come as a surprise, for on May 8, United States forces under General Zachary Taylor had already clashed with Mexican troops in the battles of Palo Alto and Resaca de la Palma. At the right, Taylor's dark-jacketed men have gone on to lay siege to the Bishop's Palace in Monterrey, Mexico, on September 22. A second assault group under General John Wool leaves San Antonio (below) for Mexico on September 26. Both paintings are by Samuel Chamberlain, who served in the American army during the war, sketching what he saw.

Antonio Lopez de Santa Anna was Mexico's military dictator and leading general during the war with the United States.

THE WAR IN CALIFORNIA

ROBERT F. STOCKTON

STEPHEN W. KEARNY

JOHN D. SLOAT

American forces at La Mesa, California (above), stop a charge by Mexican lancers on January 9, 1847. The Americans were soldiers from General Stephen W. Kearny's party who had made a grueling march of over 900 miles from Santa Fe, New Mexico, to California, and sailors and marines of Commodore John D. Sloat's Pacific squadron, who had landed in Monterey, California, in July, 1846, and marched south under the command of Commodore Robert F. Stockton. One of the Mexican army's expert lancers is shown below.

ZACHARY TAYLOR AT BUENA VISTA

In this Chamberlain painting, General Taylor (center), seated on his horse Old Whitey, commands his American forces on February 22, 1847, at the hard-fought battle of Buena Vista. His victory here made him a national hero.

The flags at the right all flew during the Mexican War. The banner at the top is the national flag of Mexico; it was taken in battle by American troops. Each of the United States regiments had its own flag that the troops followed into battle: At the center are the colors of the Fourth Regiment of Indiana Volunteers; at the bottom, the flag carried by the United States Eighth Infantry Regiment.

SMITHSONIAN INSTITUTION

SAN JACINTO MUSEUM OF HISTORY ASSOCIATION

WEST POINT MUSEUM

571

WAR IN THE WEST

THE ROAD TO MEXICO CITY

This cartoon pictures Santa Anna (left) and Mexican General Valentin Canalizo fleeing after the battle of Cerro Gordo.

WINFIELD SCOTT

The Mexican port city of Veracruz, considered by many military strategists to be the key to the capture of Mexico City, suffered a three-day bombardment (above) in March, 1847, before surrendering to the Americans. The shelling was backed up by a United States fleet of 200 ships and by nearly 14,000 troops under the command of General Winfield Scott. The Americans prepared for their siege by putting men ashore to build gun emplacements, thus adding to the firepower of the naval guns. The shore operation was directed by a young officer, Captain Robert E. Lee. Tough Mexican guerrilla fighters like the man opposite harassed the Americans manning the gun emplacements.

OVERLEAF: At Molino del Rey, Scott's army fought its last battle before the direct assault on Mexico City. Lying on the outskirts of the capital, the fortified stone buildings housed a foundry for the casting of cannon and a store of gunpowder. American intelligence had underestimated the size of the garrison defending the city; it was taken by the Americans only after both sides had met heavy casualties.

THE FINAL BATTLE
AT CHAPULTEPEC

American troops (below) begin to breach the walls guarding Chapultepec, a hill south of Mexico City that contained a complex of buildings, including the Governor's Palace. On September 13, 1847, the Americans took the hill. James Walker, who painted this panoramic canvas in 1857, probably based his work on the sketches he made while the battle was in progress.

Among the last defenders of Chapultepec were Los Niños (the boys), cadets of the Mexican Military Academy that was housed in the palace. The boys (one is shown in his uniform at the right) became a symbol to the Mexicans of their country's bravery. General Jose Mariano Monterde, commandant of the academy at the time of the siege, is shown opposite.

Mexico fell to the Americans on September 14, 1847, when General Scott and

his army rode in triumph into the great plaza in the heart of Mexico City.

CHAPTER 20

THE "SOUTHERN PROBLEM"

To Americans of the 1850s, the complications of sectionalism were so varied and so subtle that the man on the street probably had little understanding of the growing division of his nation. The issues had emerged slowly, as the nation expanded westward, and there had developed a vast economic empire loosely held together by a rather weak political allegiance. Each section paid fealty to the federal government, but each had decided opinions about its own role and its own rights.

By 1861, the South had come to regard itself not only as a distinct section but as an independent nation, willing to fight for its freedom. This development was largely mental and emotional, for there were few geographical reasons for such an argument. Except that the area had a climate warm enough to grow cotton and other semitropical crops, there was nothing to make it a natural empire. Within this warm belt there were wide topographical and climatic differences.

The auctioneer has put a young girl up for sale while the other members of her family wait their turn in this 1852 painting.

The South had few of the attributes of a well-rounded economy, or of one with any real promise of economic independence. Of all sections in the Union, it was perhaps most dependent upon the others.

It might be argued that the social structure, characterized by the master-slave relationship, so dominated the South as to give it a unity. But nowhere in the nation were there wider social differences, and as the years passed, these became increasingly apparent. As long as cheap land had been available on the frontiers, the same general set of opportunities had been open to the white settler. But with the passing of a frontier economy and the emergence of a dominant mercantile or propertied class, both business and society became less flexible. No longer was it so easy to move from one class to another. Particularly difficult to enter was the new ruling class. Because it controlled most of the land and most of the money, it was the most powerful.

Thus class lines of the South became sharply defined. Wealthy planters ran political, social, and economic affairs, for the most part. Beneath them were the smaller planters and some of the more successful professional men. Then came a group of merchants and mechanics, rather small in number, who held themselves to be above the ordinary small white farmer. Next to last were the "poor whites," often the tillers of marginal lands. Finally, at the very bottom of the scale, were the slaves.

During the first half of the 19th century, the widening gap in Southern society created problems that would be more visible in a later day. Planters who took advantage of the availability of cheap land and expanded their operations during a period of rising cotton prices became ever more powerful in the over-all economic picture. Mass production of cotton by slave labor not only drove off many of the poor whites who were unable to compete, but stunted the growth of a middle class so necessary to any economy. Few young Southerners of that day were inclined to become store owners, manufacturers, or even professional men when the returns from cotton culture were so much greater. Cotton was not only becoming king, it was also developing into something of a tyrant. To understand how this happened, it is necessary to go back in time, to colonial days.

How cotton became king

The early planters had not regarded cotton as a particularly important product. Theirs was the long-staple, or Sea Island, cotton, easily separated from its seeds, which was raised principally along a narrow coastal strip and on the offshore islands.

The vast interior uplands of the South were best suited for *short*-staple cotton. This type was hardier, yielded more pounds per acre, and could be raised in a large part of the Southern United States. But it had one major limitation: Its tight boll prevented the quick, easy separation of lint from the seed.

How this upland, short-staple cotton came to be the very lifeblood of the South resulted from the chance meeting of Eli Whitney, a New Englander recently graduated from Yale, and the widow of General Nathanael Greene. She invited him to visit her at her Georgia plantation. There he became interested in cotton separation, and by the spring of 1793, his Yankee ingenuity had produced a small gin that would perform the operation mechanically. Hand-operated, it would do the work of 10 men; by applying power, its productivity was increased

An overseer watches his slaves at work in a water color by Benjamin Henry Latrobe

Arise! Arise! and weep no more
dry up your tears, we shall part
no more. Come rose we go to
Tennessee,
that happy Shore. to old virginia
never — never — return. —

COLLECTION OF RICHARD M. KAIN

A score of Virginia slaves, sold by their masters, perhaps because of a season of poor crops and a need for cash, are on their way to new owners in Tennessee.

fivefold. The machine was simplicity itself: two rollers equipped with wire teeth tore the cotton away from the seed, dropping the latter into a box. A revolving brush, applied to the wire-studded rollers from an opposite direction, removed the cotton from the wire. In the spring of 1794 the machine was patented, an act that afforded the inventor little protection, for it was a contrivance that easily could be reproduced by any mechanic. And reproduced it was—by the thousands. Whitney's gin was the key that unlocked the door to a whole new economic empire.

The South had the right type of land, it had the cotton gin, and just now another important factor appeared—demand. The Industrial Revolution was changing England's economy, as it would that of the Northern United States. By the time the Napoleonic Wars and the War of 1812 were over, the English demand for cotton became almost insatiable. The American South was the largest and best acreage for growing cotton profitably, and to it the manufacturers of cotton products turned for their raw materials. Southerners responded to the demand, and its accompanying high prices, by attempting to produce every ounce of cotton their lands would grow.

The period 1815–40 saw the rapid expansion of the plantation system and a tremendous demand for labor to work the newly developed acreages. The backbreaking toil of raising this crop required a large, cheap labor force, and the sudden growth of a cotton empire made slavery look like a necessity to the Southern economy. Ironically, this happened just after Congress, in 1807, had voted to abolish the importation of slaves from Africa. This meant that the slave supply was restricted to those already in America, to their children, and to those

The levee at New Orleans is filled with the produce that will be loaded onto boats for the journey upriver. At the right is a somewhat idyllic painting of a cotton plantation. In reality, small farms greatly outnumbered the large ones.

who could be smuggled in. The supply was not great enough and the price of black laborers soared. Between the end of the War of 1812 and the outbreak of the Civil War, the cotton kingdom emerged. In its westward sweep, cotton culture moved as far across the South as climatic conditions would permit, stopping only when it reached the more arid parts of Texas. The results were spectacular. Production soared from 150,000 bales a year in 1812 to 4,500,000 at the time of the Civil War. In 1800, $5,000,000 worth of cotton had been exported—7% of the nation's total. By 1860, the figure was $191,000,000—57% of the value of all American exports. Cotton production tended to minimize all other forms of economic endeavor in the South, so attractive and easy were its profits. Stories were circulated to the effect that returns as high as 35% per year could be expected on investments in cotton lands.

The growth of the cotton kingdom supplied America with its best ex-ample, to that time, of *ex*tensive agriculture. Instead of working the land *in*tensively—that is, with great quantities of labor, fertilizer, and cultivation—cotton farmers tilled as much land as they could with a minimum of labor, or, to use the technical term, "extensively." It was in the American agricultural tradition to be wasteful of land, but never before had it been "mined" on such a broad scale.

In long-range terms, such ruthless extraction proved to be expensive. Just as mining takes all and returns nothing, Southern farming left little in its wake but great quantities of worn-out land incapable of real production of any kind. No one was concerned about it then, in the face of enormous profits and with the apparently unlimited supply of land. Later generations would learn the lessons of soil exhaustion.

Not all cotton was raised on large plantations, but because the cost could be lowered by mass-production methods, there was a tendency to farm on

as wide a scale as possible. Plantations ranging from 1,000 to 1,500 acres were common, especially in the newer cotton-growing regions of the West. By 1850, there were about 75,000 cotton farms designated by federal census takers as plantations.

Important as cotton was, it was not the only factor that set the South apart. Time and tradition had contributed heavily to the feeling of sectionalism. At the time of the Constitutional Convention, such Southerners as Charles Pinckney, Patrick Henry, and James Madison made reference to the South, implying that it had a set of interests separate from those of the North. What they really meant was that its characteristics arose from its agrarian background, rather than from any geographical differences or sense of nationalism. Before 1830, however, there was no real feeling among Southerners that their land was a *section* with interests of its own.

The South defends slavery

Historically, it is often difficult to fix a specific time when any new trend begins, but it may well be that 1831–32 was the conscious turning point in the thinking of the South. The slave insurrection of August, 1831, led by Nat Turner, shocked a great many white Southerners, and strengthened their belief that black people were a danger to them. The uprising, which cost 57 white lives, was crushed, but this was small satisfaction to those who already were fearful of the growing black population.

After the Turner insurrection,

Most of the familiar ingredients of the popular, romantic conception of life as it was along the Mississippi are found in this Currier and Ives print.

Southerners stopped apologizing for the "peculiar institution" and began to fashion a set of proslavery arguments in defense of it. Their determination was heightened by the appearance of William Lloyd Garrison's radical paper, *The Liberator,* and the abolitionist charges of Southern sin arising out of the institution of slavery. Forgotten were the stories of how George Washington and John Randolph had freed their slaves, by will; of Thomas Jefferson's efforts gradually to rid the South of slavery; and of Patrick Henry or James Madison, who had suggested emancipation. Instead, there were now warnings about what would happen to Southern civilization should the slaves be freed, and pronouncements about the natural superiority of whites over blacks. Those favoring slavery maintained that their system was one of benevolence and humanity compared to the plight of the wage slaves of the New England factories. They searched the classics and the Bible for citations supporting the natural relationship between master and slave. No arguments were overlooked by believers in slavery in their search to justify an institution that many Southerners wanted to abandon.

As a result, some Southerners were converted from a defensive position to the stand that slavery was a positive good. Thomas Roderick Dew, a young William and Mary College professor, began his published refutations of emancipation in 1832. By the 1850s,

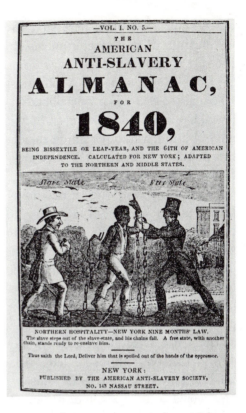

During the prewar period, antislavery propaganda was even found in almanacs.

a number of other essayists had joined him, and as the literary volume mounted in intensity, the tone of the writings became increasingly militant. Senator James Hammond of South Carolina went so far as to denounce the doctrine of equality of men in the Declaration of Independence. When such public figures as Hammond and John C. Calhoun took up their cudgels, the argument was transferred from the literary field to politics. Once this step was taken, there was little possibility of Southern retreat.

Partly as a defense against the outcries of Northern abolitionists, partly out of sheer economic necessity, the justification of slavery continued. (In 1860, the value of slaves was some $2,000,000,000, and no abolitionist who insisted that this property be outlawed had been able to suggest how it might be done without ruining the entire Southern economy.) It was a vicious circle. Ironically, some of the same Southerners who were doing their best to justify slavery and to push their section toward secession were unwittingly preserving the conditions that would make it impossible for the South to win its fight for independence. The quest for ever-larger profits in cotton had fastened slavery on the South, which kept it essentially a rural society, without skilled workers, and prevented the rise of industry. This would cost the South dearly in the Civil War.

Slavery splits the Democrats

In politics, as might be assumed, Southern leaders were by nature conservative, and became more so as the Civil War neared. The Whig Party seemed to be the logical place for them, but its advocacy of nationalism ran counter to their growing feeling of sectionalism. And the Whigs' growing support of a high tariff was another disturbing development to the agricultural South. Even this might have been tolerated had the Whigs taken a strong stand upon the slavery issue. When they did not, Southerners were thrown into the arms of the Democratic Party. By 1860, the party of

Jackson had secured itself as the party of the conservative South.

The acceptance of the party by the Southerners contributed to its division at the national level. When Southerners tried to force Kansas into the Union as a slave state under the Lecompton Constitution, against the will of a majority of its people, and when aggressive Southerners began to demand "positive protection" of slavery in all the territories, a bitter quarrel broke out between President James Buchanan, on the Southern side, and Stephen A. Douglas, on the Northern. This divided the Democratic Party in two. Thousands of Northern Democrats came to regard it as the "slave party" and at once began to search for new political allegiances. The Democratic Party, an unwilling victim of guilt by association with slavery, was ripped apart as a prelude to division of the nation.

It was the Southern leaders, many of them from the plantation class, who led their section down the path of political secession almost a decade before independence was declared. Fearing the growing dominance of the North, they were willing to risk dissolution of the Union rather than surrender their disproportionate place of importance in national affairs. By the time actual hostilities began, the South had convinced itself that it had a destiny of its own. Emotions took command and there was a general outbreak of sectional fervor. By then, few questioned its origins.

WHALERS AND CLIPPERS

There were two great periods for American sailing vessels, both of them ending shortly after the Civil War. Whaling began in the 17th century, based mainly in the Bay Colony, then on Long Island and Nantucket, and finally at New Bedford, Massachusetts, but it was not until around 1820 that this country's fleet was greater than that of the British and became the master of the whaling industry. With the increased supply of petroleum and the destruction of the whaling fleet in the Civil War, the industry went into decline. The clipper ships started to rule the seas around 1845, taking goods to and from the Orient, miners to the gold fields of California, and farmers to the lands of Australia. They existed without competition from any other ships in speed and power, and they continued to do so until steam-operated vessels came into general use. So the history of the whalers and clippers is short, but it is an exciting history—one filled with physical hardships, travel to distant and strange lands, and adventures fighting the seas. Both produced wealth that quickly came and went, but for a long time was important in making the young nation strong financially and as a sea power. Although their heyday is more than a century past, each has left behind stories that have grown into legends of the days when American whalers and clippers sailed the world.

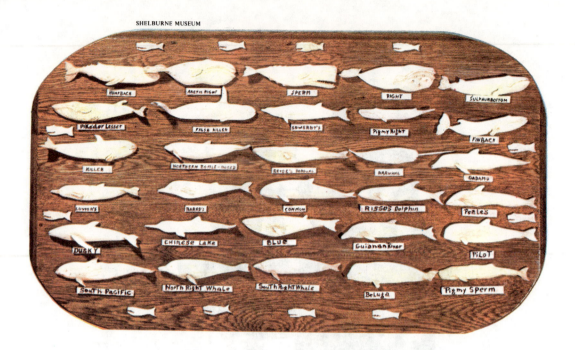

The carved miniatures are labeled: HUMPBACK, ARCTIC RIGHT, SPERM, RIGHT, SULPHURBOTTOM, PIKED or LESSER, FALSE KILLER, SOWERBY'S, Pigmy Right, FINBACK, KILLER, NORTHERN BOTTLE-NOSED, BRYDE'S RORQUAL, NARWHAL, GADAMU, KUVIER'S, BAIRD'S, COMMON, RISSO'S Dolphin, PEALES, DUSKY, CHINESE LAKE, BLUE, Guianan River, PILOT, South Pacific, North Right Whale, South Right Whale, Beluga, Pigmy Sperm

WHALERS AND CLIPPERS

THE CAPITAL

The great days of whaling came to New Bedford, Massachusetts, from 1825–60. Out of its harbor (right) went hundreds of ships, and its streets were full of shops for their equipment—sailmakers, riggers, ropemakers, blacksmiths, carpenters. Atop Johnnycake Hill stood the Seaman's Bethel (left), a church for whalemen, and not far away, but still a distance from the waterfront and the smell of whale oil, were the mansions of the rich merchants. These men financed the ships, but their actual operation was in the hands of stern and just New England seamen like the two New Bedford whaling captains at the right above. The captains had to be hard taskmasters, for whaling was a dangerous business that fought against great odds to bring about great profits. Above are a series of carved miniatures of various whales, the awesome mammals that were responsible for this short-lived but exciting maritime industry.

590

STEPHEN C. CHRISTIAN

THOMAS NYE, JR.

PREPARATION

Most whalers carried three or four boats, each with a crew of six and a captain or mate acting as headsman. The whaleboat above is an accurate model made to scale.

1 *Harpoon*	15 *Blubber-hook*
2 *Lance*	16 *Horse Gaff*
3 *Head Spade*	17 *Mincing Knife*
4 *Boat Spade*	18 *Check-Pin, Boat*
5 *Boarding Knife*	19 *Case Bucket*
6 *Cutting-in-Spade*	20 *Waif* Bt
7 *Raised Pike*	21 *Boat Hook*
8 *Gaff Head*	22 *Drug*
9 *Pike*	23 *Compass*
10 *Fork*	24 *Buoy*
11 *Bailer*	25 *Hatchet* Bt
12 *Skimmer*	26 *Knife*
13 *Toggle*	27 *Line Tub*
14 *Cutting Block*	28 *Water Keg*
29 *Bucket* Bt	31 *Crotch*
30 *Lantern Keg*	32 *Fin Chain*
34 *Needle*	33 *Monkey Rope*	35 *Lantern*

Whalers were equipped with most of the implements shown above. The drawing is from a journal kept by John F. Martin while he was on a voyage aboard the *Lucy Ann* in 1841. The crew at the right has worked itself up to the whale and is about to throw the harpoon—the moment when the months of preparation are tested.

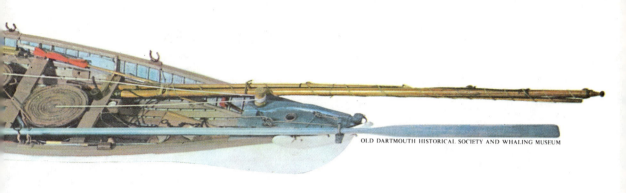

AFTER THE HARPOONING

In the early days of whaling, the right whale was the one most often harpooned. With a large tongue and no teeth, it was recognized at a distance by its great forked spray. The sperm whale was discovered around 1700. It was bigger than the right whale and fought more fiercely with its enormous jaw and giant teeth, but his blubber made oil of finer quality. After the whale was harpooned, the blubber was stripped from its sides (left) and then cut up and boiled in the try-pots (above), from which the oil was taken. Below is an old logbook recording the whales sighted (left) and those taken (right).

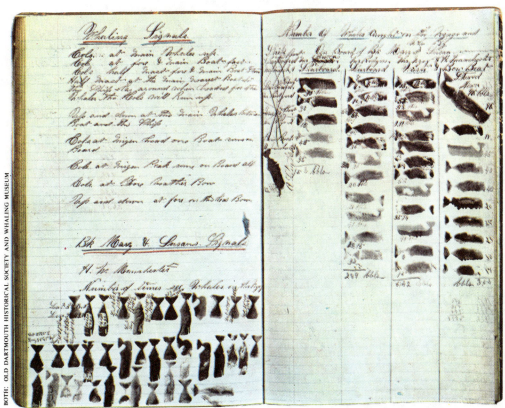

FAR TRAVEL

As the whalers moved farther from their home port for their catch, they entered areas never before or seldom seen by white men. At the left is a native as he was seen on the Sandwich Islands—the former name of the Hawaiian Islands. Below is a whaler's view of one of the Cape Verde Islands, owned by Portugal. It was here captains got Portuguese sailors, who later settled in New Bedford.

Whaling developed its legends, one of which is about John Tabor, who rode with an old man whaleback across the ocean and up the main street of his town.

OVERLEAF: This 1850 lithograph shows a sperm whale coming up under a boat, splitting it in two, and throwing the crew into a churning sea to fight for their lives.

DONALD MCKAY

CLIPPERS

There is an endless argument about when the first clipper ship appeared, but that she was built in America sometime between 1835 and 1845 is agreed upon. With a hull designed for speed and heavily sparred to allow for her many sails, she was the fastest ship ever to sail up to that time. The glory of the clipper was short: Donald McKay (left), one of the great builders in 1855, is shown in the photograph inspecting his last clipper in 1869.

The *Sea Witch* began by carrying large cargoes at high speed to China, and ended by taking coolie laborers to Cuba. She was one of the fastest clippers, breaking and setting more records than any sailing ship of her size, before or since.

TO THE ORIENT

PEABODY MUSEUM

The clippers were first built to sail to the Orient, and in particular to the city of Canton. To limit the Westerners' influence, it was the only port the Chinese opened to them. There the clippers traded with the Co-Hong, an organization of merchants set up by the government. This group made ships anchor at Whampoa (below), a dozen miles downstream from Canton, and placed all quarters for the shippers in an area outside Canton's walls.

TRAVELERS WEST

AUSTRALIA !

Mailler, Lord & Quereau's "Kangaroo Line"

FOR MELBOURNE.

First Vessel, sailing promptly on Advertised Day.

THE SPLENDID FIRST CLASS CLIPPER SHIP

JACK FROST

1,000 Tons Register, G. T. EMERY, Commander,

Insuring strictly A 1, is now rapidly loading at **Pier 10 East River,** and will have early and prompt dispatch for

MELBOURNE, DIRECT.

The accommodations for first and second class passengers are very superior.

For Freight or Passage, apply on board as above, or to

MAILLER, LORD & QUEREAU,

108 WALL STREET.

LORD & CO., Consignees at Melbourne, for whom consignments are solicited.

SIGHT BILLS for sale, and advances made on approved shipments.

NESBITT & CO., PRINTERS.

SEAMEN'S BANK FOR SAVINGS, NEW YORK CITY

When gold came to California in 1849, it also came to the owners of the clipper ships, who supplied the main source of transportation to the boom town of San Francisco. Shippers built at a frantic rate, and in 1853 over 125 vessels were launched—some of these to take emigrants to places like Australia (left).

The Confederate cruiser *Nashville* destroys a clipper from a Northern port in 1862, an

he action symbolizes the end of wind-driven ships before the new power of steam.

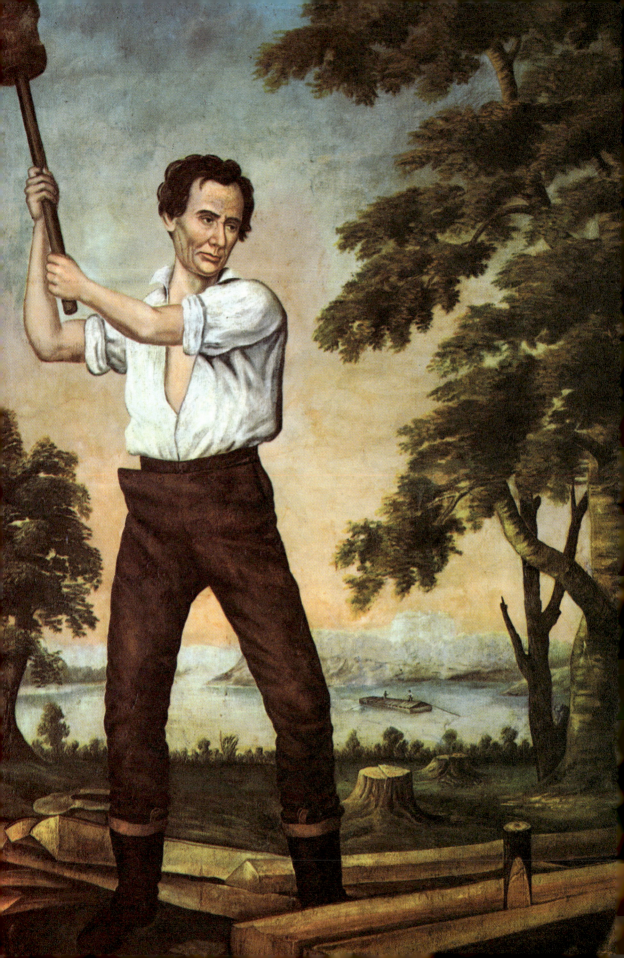

THE ROAD TO DISUNION

By the summer of 1860, the political division of the United States was complete. Already Jefferson Davis had recommended a dissolution of the Union should a Republican be elected as a result of the campaign that year. Robert A. Toombs, a prominent Georgian, warned his countrymen against letting the nation fall into the hands of the "Black Republican Party." Amidst such threats, the Republicans met at Chicago and on the third ballot nominated Abraham Lincoln as their candidate, to the bitter disappointment of William H. Seward.

The turmoil of sectionalism was well demonstrated by the Democrats' dilemma in 1860. Northern party members were determined to support Senator Douglas and his theories on popular sovereignty, and the Southerners were equally determined to repudiate him. The Northern faction succeeded in getting control of the convention in Charleston, South Carolina, and putting across a pro-Douglas platform. The anti-Douglas

What is reputed to have been a campaign banner of 1860 shows Lincoln in the role that his supporters wanted to stress.

men, frustrated in their efforts to get a platform advocating protection of slavery in the territories, finally walked out of the convention. Douglas' supporters retreated to Baltimore, where they met anew, only to engage in another fierce debate that resulted in the departure of more Southerners for home. What was left of the convention then nominated Stephen A. Douglas for President and Herschel V. Johnson of Georgia for Vice-President.

The Southern Democrats promptly nominated John C. Breckinridge as their candidate for President and an Oregonian, Joseph Lane, as his running mate. A fourth party, largely composed of former Whigs and Know Nothings, took the name Constitutional Union and nominated conservative John Bell of Tennessee and Edward Everett of Massachusetts.

The campaign that followed was characterized by interparty struggles within the sections rather than a conflict between North and South. In the North, the contest was largely Lincoln against Douglas, while in the South the battle was between Breckinridge and Bell. Douglas took the stump for the preservation of the Union and for a program favoring the common man —a stand that had a wide appeal and one hard to oppose. Lincoln did relatively little campaigning, letting his supporters march in torchlight parades, hold rallies, and in general put on a campaign reminiscent of the old Whig "hurrah" methods. The Republicans played down the issue of slavery wherever they could, and talked about homesteads for the people and tariff protection for business interests. They made their appeal to the antislavery elements just strong enough to make the abolitionists feel that the new party represented their best hope for the end of the "peculiar institution." And they appealed to Eastern conservatives by condemning corruption in the Buchanan administration.

In the South, the campaign was one for and against secession. To the fire-eaters, this was the final crisis, the last of a long series of encroachments by the North, and there was no other answer for them but to leave the Union. Southern moderates answered that there had been no overt actions on the part of the North, that the South had not really suffered any grievous wrongs, and that a Republican victory might be bad, but it certainly would not be fatal. They held that Southern rights could be better preserved in the Union than out, that secession was just another word for revolution.

Northerners tended to disregard the threats that secession would follow a Lincoln victory. Senator William Fessenden of Maine told his people that

"Ain't you glad you joined the Republicans?" sang this excited group in 1860 as they marched down New York City's Broadway in a mammoth torchlight parade.

such threats were made merely to frighten off Republican voters, while Edward Bates of Missouri, soon to be in Lincoln's cabinet, called them "all brag and bluster." Young Charles Francis Adams, on tour with his famous father and with Senator Seward that summer, tried to assess the magnitude of the coming danger. Later he admitted that they had all lived in a fool's paradise, and he expressed amazement, in retrospect, over their blindness to the possible consequences of Lincoln's election. "We knew nothing of the South," he wrote, "had no realizing sense of the intensity of the feeling which there prevailed; we fully believed it would all end in gasconade."

As it turned out, Lincoln was a minority President. He polled only 1,866,352 popular votes against a total of 2,814,519 for his combined opponents. The larger figure, however, was divided as follows: Douglas, 1,375,157; Breckinridge, 849,781; and Bell, 589,581. In the electoral college, Lincoln polled 180 votes while the others totaled 123.

When the returns were in, a nervous calm fell across the nation. The Republicans, still a minority party in the fall of 1860, had elected a minority President who would have to wait four months before he could take any official action in the secession crisis. For more than a decade, Southerners had talked of leaving the Union, and since the rise of the Republican Party they had openly threatened to walk out if a Republican were elected President.

Still, Northerners continued to ignore such talk and joked among themselves that there were enough jails and asylums to house all secessionists. Lincoln himself had said, in 1856, that "all this talk about the dissolution of the Union is humbug—nothing but folly. We won't dissolve the Union, and you shan't." Even in the autumn of 1860, after the election was past, most Northerners thought their Southern friends were bluffing. But as the weeks wore on, the awful suspicion began to grow that perhaps matters were more serious than had been imagined. Even Thurlow Weed, the New York politician, stopped joking about the possible secession of Coney Island.

Matters were complicated by the fact that the period between the election and Lincoln's inauguration constituted an executive interregnum. Buchanan was unwilling to take any action that would create more problems for his successor, and Lincoln was, until March 4, 1861, a private citizen. Old Buck, as Buchanan was known, was no strong man, and if the South took aggressive action, it was unlikely that he would act positively in any event.

All this worried the country, and the only solace the supporters of the Union could find in the situation was that the South itself, for the moment, was leaderless and somewhat undecided as to the course it should take. The South had two alternatives: It could recognize the results of the recent election and try to work within the framework of established government, as before, seeking some solution to its grievances; or the individual states could secede and perhaps form some organization of their own. Those who lived in the northern part of the South, in the border states, inclined toward the first alternative. In the Deep South, there were moderates who felt the same way. They hoped time would heal the wound, that Lincoln's known moderation would prevail over the more radical elements, both North and South. The secessionists, of course, believed that severance from the Union was the only proper course.

Lincoln's taciturnity after the election worried many Americans, North and South. Many a Yankee who had voted for him was anxious to learn what he was going to do about the threatened secession; Southerners were equally interested, and his continued silence deepened their distrust of him. But Lincoln rightly felt that he had already made his nonaggressive position on slavery, and his firm position on maintenance of the Union, quite clear. He believed that making new statements about his intentions would lead to misinterpretations that would have to be followed by more explanations. He did not want to entangle himself in such a web before becoming President. Even Seward, the firebrand, counseled caution, and no more was heard from him about an "irrepressible conflict." His attitudes were important and were watched

closely, because prior to March 4, 1861, Seward was "Mr. Republican," the best known man in his party.

Despite the remark by one of Lincoln's fellow Republicans that he hoped the President-elect would not open his mouth "save only to eat, until March 4," the tall man from Illinois found a relatively safe means of expressing himself on the burning issues of the day. He had long talks with his friend Senator Lyman Trumbull of Illinois, appeared at public gatherings with him, and even wrote part of one of his speeches. Speaking through Trumbull, he tried to allay the Southerners' fears, assuring them that he intended to protect property (that is, slaves). He wanted to convey his attitude of moderation and conservatism. Another method Lincoln used, on advice of his followers, was to send out feelers to prominent Southerners to learn if they would serve in his cabinet. He corresponded with Alexander Stephens of Georgia, soon to be Vice-President of the Confederacy, but Stephens ended the overture when he expressed himself strongly on the sectional issue. There were also negotiations between Lincoln and John Gilmer, former Congressman from North Carolina, but nothing came of them.

Meanwhile, early in December, Buchanan delivered his annual message to Congress. In general terms he urged a peaceful settlement of the controversy, with perhaps a constitutional amendment to guarantee South-

The cartoonist jibes at Lincoln, dancing to Horace Greeley's tune, with lips locked about slavery, which William Seward (background) says is the issue to be faced. Below, the poster gives the Republican view of the 1860 campaign issues.

Alexander H. Stephens

John J. Crittenden

erners their slave properties and to offer them similar protection in federal territories. Senator John Crittenden of Kentucky and Senator Andrew Johnson of Tennessee—both border-state moderates—supported the compromise, and Crittenden introduced a resolution to effectuate it. He suggested that slavery be prohibited north of 36° 30′ and that it be both permitted and protected south of that line. Future states might come in with or without slavery, regardless of their location; a stronger fugitive-slave law would be enacted; and the federal government would compensate owners of runaway slaves where threat or intimidation had prevented their recovery. These proposals would be added to the Con-

stitution in the form of six amendments, with a guarantee that they would never be altered to allow Congress to change the status of slavery in any state.

The moderates fail

Lincoln was willing to make some concessions, but was not impressed by Crittenden's proposals. They would leave the door wide open for the forcible expansion of slavery into Cuba, Mexico, and Central America. They would foster slavery in Southwestern areas where it had never taken root. Numerous Republican Senators asked why a compromise was required when the electorate had spoken so recently. They were fearful that too moderate a stand might wreck the new party,

614

Stephens urged moderation and Crittenden worked for compromise. But the rush toward secession (caricatured above), with South Carolina in the lead, was on.

and they also watched with growing concern the advanced state of secessionist sentiment in the South.

As Congress debated and dawdled, secession finally took place. Southerners gradually concluded that Lincoln was a sectional President—a man who represented the North only—and therefore they could not receive just treatment. The fact that he had not received a single electoral vote in the Southern states strengthened this feeling. As the South Carolinians had prepared to choose their Presidential electors, their governor advised them that they must be ready to secede should Lincoln win. When the election results were known, a convention was called in South Carolina, and on December 20, 1860, it voted unan-imously to sever the state's tie with the Union.

South Carolina held itself to be an independent nation, having no allegiance to North or South. Early in January, Alabama, Florida, and Mississippi seceded, and later that month Georgia and Louisiana followed. There was no organization or plan of union among the states that had withdrawn. Each simply held itself to be independent. On February 1, 1861, Texas left the Union, despite Governor Sam Houston's vigorous attempts to prevent it. The seven seceding states met in convention in Montgomery, Alabama, on February 4, 1861. Their purpose was to form a new government to be called the Confederate States of America.

The situation was unique in American history. While states of the Deep South put together their own government, the rest of the Union stood by and watched. All eyes were on the border states, whose decision was to be enormously important. Any sudden, hostile move by the North or South would push these undecided states over to the other side.

The same day the Confederates met at Montgomery, another group of Americans gathered at Washington to try to save the Union. Twenty-one states were represented. Although the attempt came to nothing, it is significant that it was originated by the Virginia legislature, whose members were not, on February 4, ready to break away from the rest of the nation. Nor was it the fault of Southerners that the conference failed, for only one Northern state legislature—that of New Jersey—voted to support the proposed compromise. It was the final attempt at preserving the Union.

During the spring of 1861, as the nation awaited Lincoln's inauguration and an announcement of the new administration's policy, the feeling of nervous excitement mounted. During this time, federal forts and other government property in the South fell into the hands of the Confederacy. Buchanan stood by, apparently helpless, and made no move to intervene. Northerners watched the transfer with annoyance and wondered what, if anything, the new administration would do about it. There were some who thought nothing should be done—that the seceded states should be allowed to depart in peace and come home again after they had thought out their problems. On the other hand, many Northern conservatives felt that the Union should be preserved at all costs—even war. Both points of view, divergent as they were, militated against compromise.

At the outer edges of political thought stood the radicals—the Southerners who were secessionists, the Northerners who were for maintenance of the Union by the most determined action. These were the two divergent groups that made turning back an impossibility.

For those on either side of the issue who had doubts, events began to bring the crisis into sharper focus. During the early months of 1861, a number of federal forts in the South were taken over by secessionist forces. Fort Pulaski in Georgia fell in January. So did Fort Morgan and Fort Gaines in Alabama. At Pensacola, Florida, the federal navy yard changed hands. And in Texas some 19 posts were handed over without a struggle before that state had ratified its ordinance of secession. Supporters of the Union watched these losses with growing dismay, wondering if the process would be completed without objection from the federal government.

The inauguration of Jefferson Davis as Confederate President took place on February 18, 1861, in Montgomery, Alabama.

617

Robert Anderson   *P.G.T. Beauregard*

All eyes soon turned upon Fort Sumter in Charleston harbor, and the nation watched to see what the newly inaugurated President would do when the pressure was put on there. This little bastion, perched on a small island in the heart of secession land, became a symbol—a test case. The President had pledged in his inaugural speech that he would do everything in his power to "hold, occupy, and possess" federal property that lay within Confederate territory. And chiefly that meant Fort Sumter. What would happen if the federal government refused to give it up? Would there be war, or would the Southerners back down? These and many other questions crossed American minds in the tense weeks that followed Lincoln's inauguration.

The answer was not long in coming. The new President made it clear that he intended to uphold the law of the land—and that included the defense of federal property. Sumter would be provisioned and maintained. The new Confederate government, with temporary headquarters at Montgomery, now faced its first challenge. After some debate, it was decided that South Carolina must be supported: The fort would be destroyed. Despite the anguished pleas of the Confederate Secretary of State, Robert A. Toombs, who said, "It is suicide, murder, and will lose us every friend in the North," orders went out to General P. G. T. Beauregard at Charleston to bombard the fort into submission. That was on April 11.

Major Robert Anderson, commanding the fort, rejected South Carolina's demands for surrender, but admitted he would be forced to comply within a few days, when he would run out of supplies. Unwilling to wait, and certain that the federal government intended to reinforce the post, Beauregard ordered the bombardment to

On April 12, 1861, with the firing on Fort Sumter, the Civil War began. Anderson was the federal commander, Beauregard headed the Confederate attack.

start. At 4:30 a.m. on April 12, the Civil War began.

Sumter surrenders to the rebels

By the following morning, Sumter was crumbling and fire had broken out in the magazine. Anderson called for a cease-fire, agreeing to formal evacuation on Sunday, April 14. As suddenly as they had begun, the hostilities in Charleston harbor ended. In place of flying cannon balls, wherrymen plied their gaily decorated little boats back and forth, carrying curious sightseers out to the island. At 2 p.m., Major Anderson made ready to fire a 100-gun salute in honor of his flag and to formalize the surrender. During the firing, Private Daniel Hough stuffed a powder bag into a gun that had not been properly swabbed, and in the premature explosion he lost his life. Five other men were wounded, and one of them died later. Thus, after a bombardment that had cost Anderson none of his men, Private Hough became the Civil War's first casualty, because of carelessness in firing a salute to the flag.

The next morning, the Fort Sumter garrison boarded the steamer *Baltic* and headed north. Probably surprised at not being held prisoner, the men must have wondered what the next step would be in the strange war that had started at Charleston. How would the North react to the fort's surrender? Would the little unpleasantness that had begun in the harbor be carried forward? Or would the South be allowed to go its own way? If these were the thoughts in the soldiers' minds, they were not alone in having them. Millions, North and South, asked the same questions, recalling Lincoln's inaugural address. In grave words he had reminded the South that he had taken "the most solemn" oath to "preserve, protect, and defend" the Union.

MAIN TEXT CONTINUES IN VOLUME 8

Daniel Webster: Great Man Eloquent

A SPECIAL CONTRIBUTION BY

GERALD W. JOHNSON

Today a legendary figure, Daniel Webster is not remembered so much for his legal victories or his terms as Secretary of State as for his eloquent words on liberty and union.

For more than 100 years everybody has been writing about Daniel Webster and some have written well, but it can be plausibly argued that only one has written truthfully. There are 12 formal lives of Webster listed in the *Dictionary of American Biography,* and this takes no account of shorter studies by historians, philosophers, journalists, orators, and every known brand of politician. Few Americans have been more assiduously studied over so long a period.

But if effective history is such knowledge of the past as modifies contemporary thought and action, then one must agree with William A. Dunning that truth in history is not necessarily what happened, but what men *believe* happened, for it is on their beliefs that they act. What the vast majority of Americans believe about Daniel Webster is only slightly related to the mass of documentary evidence that scholarship has turned up, but it is not on that account to be dismissed as untrue. Fact and truth are related, but they are not

To the conservatives of New England, Webster was known as "godlike Daniel," a man who supported their causes with granite strength.

identical, which accounts for our ability to weld "sophist" and "moron" into one word—the eternal sophomore who may acquire massive factual knowledge, but whom truth eludes.

The pedestrian writers who have dealt with Webster—even Gamaliel Bradford the Younger, even Samuel Hopkins Adams—have been hamstrung by their reliance on demonstrable fact as the key to essential truth. Not until the man had been almost a century dead did one who was no pedestrian, but a rider on Pegasus, have the boldness to repudiate fact altogether and present Webster not as he was prior to 1852, but as he is now.

There was indeed a Senator named Webster who represented Massachusetts, but he is dead. There was a fabulously successful corporation lawyer, but he, too, is dead, and who cares? There was a man, curiously compounded of wisdom and folly, who suffered adulation for his folly and denunciation for his wisdom, who tried to understand this world and failed, as we all do, and who, as we all must, eventually died.

There never was, in visible, tangible flesh, a man who performed the feats attributed to the hero of Stephen Vincent Benet's allegory, *The Devil and Daniel Webster*. The story asserts that this advocate, as counsel for the defense in the case of *Satan vs. Jabez Stone,* won a verdict and, incidentally, his own salvation from a jury composed of the 12 greatest villains in American history, because the advocate's fiery patriotism burned away his client's and his own offenses. Nevertheless, in the eyes of posterity this fictional pleader has been the living Webster rather than the subject of the 12 biographies.

For the poet Benet did not create this figure any more than the poet Homer created the figure of Achilles. Like Homer,

'E'd 'eard men sing by land and sea;
An' what 'e thought 'e might require,
'E went an' took—

to distill it in the alembic of poetic art and produce the Immortal. He gathered up the pre-existing legends and traditions, stripped off their crudity, and added grace and dignity to a figure that the folk imagination had limned before Benet was born. But in so doing he revealed the potency of Daniel Webster in the modern world more precisely than any factual historian has revealed it.

The potency does not rest upon the statutes Webster drew, the contracts he negotiated, or the politics he played. It is based upon his success as the establisher of moods, and that kind of success is never attested by documents. On the contrary, the documentary evidence often seems to contradict it, which is so much the worse for the documentary evidence. It is just this failure of the letter to capture the spirit that is the ruin of biographers and historians and the opportunity of poets. Talking of Daniel Webster conveys little that is of importance today; it was when Benet began to sing that the still-surviving power and glory appeared.

The industrious pedestrians have uncovered the facts down to astonishingly small details. A New Hampshire farmer, wise beyond most of his generation, spared one of his many children the hard labor of the fields because the boy was physically sickly, although mentally precocious. Instead, the boy was sent to the best teachers available and eventually to Dartmouth College. He justified this indulgence twice, first by helping one of his brothers through college, and later by abandoning a promising professional career to care for his parents in their declining years. But the lofty intelligence, like the Scriptural city set upon a hill, could not be hidden; at 31 the man was in the House of Representatives from New Hampshire. This was in 1813, just before the final wreck of the Federalist Party in the Hartford Convention at the beginning of 1815. With his party shot from under him, the young man repaired to Boston in 1816 and in 10 years had pushed his income from legal practice to $15,000 a year—in purchasing power the equivalent of about $150,000 today. He was elected a Representative again in 1823, went to the Senate in 1827 and 1844, was Secretary of State under three Presidents, and died in 1852.

Like many first-rate Americans who go into politics, he wished to be President of the United States, and like most first-rate men he suffered the mortification of seeing second-raters chosen in his stead. During his time in Washington, Webster saw 10 individuals occupying the White House and knew in his heart that he was superior to eight of them. No doubt he thought he was superior to the other two, Madison and Jackson, but history disallows that claim.

The second most brilliant period of American politics was beginning when Webster entered Congress, and he was, in popular estimation, one-third of it. That was, of course, the same kind of exaggeration that gives the most brilliant period one half to Jefferson and the other half to Hamilton, although they were merely the two brightest stars in a galaxy. In the second period, Webster, Clay, and Calhoun outshone all other members of Congress, but not by much. Benton, Hayne, John Quincy Adams, Van Buren, Marcy, and John Randolph were no dim lights, and outside of Congress stood the gigantic figures of Andrew Jackson and John Marshall.

Of the illustrious trio, Webster was the latest arrival and, on technicalities, the least successful. All of them made cabinet rank, but Calhoun was Vice-President for seven years and Clay was three times a candidate for President, twice as the nominee of a major party. Thus it may fairly be said that both came closer to the White House than Webster did, although none reached it.

Without doubt, Webster was refused even a nomination because his affiliations made him

This 1793 print is the earliest known view of New Hampshire's Dartmouth College, from which Webster was graduated and which he defended before the Supreme Court in 1819.

politically unavailable. He was the recognized spokesman of big business, and even at that early date, party leaders were sure that nomination of such a candidate would be party suicide. It was not regarded as scandalous for a member of Congress to continue to serve his rich clients even—indeed especially—before government agencies, but it was regarded as a political handicap, and Webster's party was never strong enough to assume that handicap. Curiously enough, this favorite advocate for astute businessmen had so little money sense that in spite of an income that was, for the time, a huge one, he was perpetually in debt and therefore never able to break away from subservience to wealth.

But there is another aspect of this man that is even more curious. The spokesman of big business, the great corporation lawyer, is a familiar figure. There is always at least one in Congress, frequently half a dozen in the

623

administration, and they are conspicuous, often dominant, figures, so we know the type, or think we do. And the common opinion is that the agent of big business, whatever his merits, is decidedly a cold fish, emphatically not the kind of material out of which popular heroes are made. Is it imaginable that a poet could have woven a folk tale around Thomas C. Platt or Nelson W. Aldrich or Elihu Root or Andrew Mellon? But Webster was legendary even before his death, and since then the legend has grown until it overshadows that of Henry Clay, much the more popular figure while he lived.

The inescapable inference is that there was a link between the ordinary American and this extraordinary individual—some quality that enables the common man to feel a kinship with Webster that he never feels with any cold fish. The easy assumption is that his faults endeared him to the sinful majority, and no doubt they did to some extent.

> Dan Webster stoked his boilers with brown
>   jugs of apple cider,
> And when he made a speech he yanked the
>   spigot open wider.
> Sing ho! those spirited debates, bereft of all
>   restrictions,
> When statesmen carried on their hip the
>   strength of their convictions,

is evidence that his fondness for the bottle passed into the legend, and his amorous adventures, probably apocryphal, have been the theme of innumerable smoking-room stories. But these things the people regard with indulgence, not with approval, and somewhere in the American mind there is a deep and powerful approval of Daniel Webster, and a proprietary pride.

Yet when one examines any of his specific activities, it seems far away and long ago, often without much logical significance even at the time. The celebrated *Reply to Hayne,* for example, was not a reply to Hayne at all. It was the evocation of a mood, not the refutation of an argument—a histrionic, not a logical triumph. "Liberty *and* Union, now and forever, one and inseparable!" had nothing whatever to do with the points that Hayne had

raised, but it stirred up a tremendous emotional reaction against the idea of disunion. Logic often eludes the grasp of the masses, but they understand feeling instantly, and they understood Webster. His heart was in the right place.

At least four of his exploits have affected and still affect the destinies of every man and woman in the United States, and each of them was of the same order—the establishment of a mood rather than the defense of a thesis. These were the Dartmouth College case, the case of *McCulloch vs. Maryland,* the negotiation of the Webster-Ashburton Treaty, and the Compromise of 1850.

Examined in the cold light of reason, all these are now without significance, but in the warm glow of emotion it is apparent that each of them grips us with an unbreakable hold. None was the work of Daniel Webster alone, but he was an operative force in all four, and he remains an operative force to this day.

The Dartmouth College case, finally decided by the Supreme Court, established the sanctity of contract. The case revolved around an effort by the State of New Hampshire to move in and take control of a college that had been chartered, perpetually, as a private institution. This effort, Webster argued, was an attempt by the state to repudiate a contract, which not even a sovereign has a right to do. The court presumably was convinced by the logic of the argument, but Webster's passing remark, "She is a small college, sir, but there are those that love her," hit the country with an impact that no logical exposition could have achieved. The fact that this case came close to repealing the Statutes of Mortmain and delivering the future into economic bondage was something for jurisconsults to worry over; the people felt it rescued cherished and threatened institutions, and that mood has persisted through all the discomforts that immortality of corporations has brought upon us.

The case of *McCulloch vs. Maryland,* also decided by the highest court, successfully asserted the right of judicial review of state laws. Logically it is untenable, but practically it has worked, and that is enough for the common man. Possibly the hard core of that decision was Chief Justice John Marshall's determination to bow his arrogant head to no man. That is as it may be. But deep in the heart of the common man is a conviction that logic is an invention of schoolmasters that bears precious little relation to life as he lives it. So even in this legalistic matter he felt close to Daniel Webster, and with that mood established, the feeling that the Constitution must be made to work, even it has to be bent into the shape of a pretzel, has persisted from that day to this.

The Webster-Ashburton Treaty is one of the most remarkable in the history of diplomacy—not for what is contained so much as for the manner in which it was negotiated. Alexander Baring, Lord Ashburton, was sent over in 1842 as a special envoy to take up with

On January 26, 1830, Webster took this classic stance in the United States Senate and made his famous statement, "Liberty and Union, now and forever, one and inseparable!"

Webster, then Secretary of State, a number of issues in dispute between the United States and Great Britain, the most important of which was the boundary line between Maine and Canada. That line had been properly surveyed years before, but no agreement had been reached in spite of a century of argument. The British would have liked the disputed land so they could control the road that supplied their Quebec fort. Americans wanted the land simply because they felt it was theirs.

Through Jared Sparks, who had recently been in Paris, Webster was supplied with a map said to have been marked by Benjamin Franklin and given to the French—and it knocked the bottom out of the American claim. About the same time, someone discovered in the British archives a map supposed to have been marked for King George III—and *it* knocked the bottom out of the British claim. But neither negotiator suspected the existence of the other map; each thought his own position exceedingly precarious.

Thus each went into the discussion warily and with the most scrupulous regard for punctilio. When the citizens of Maine threatened to become obstreperous, Webster privately showed their leaders a copy of the Jared Sparks map and moderated their attitude.

But much more was accomplished than the boundary settlement—much that does not appear in the written records and, indeed, was never formally admitted by either side. This was a marked softening of our diplomatic contacts with Great Britain. His lordship discovered that the American, far from being a raucous and semiliterate backwoodsman, was an urbane and gentlemanly fellow. The American, on his part, discovered that a noble lord is not necessarily arrogant and supercilious, but may be a reasonable, fair-minded person with whom it is a pleasure to do business. The discovery that each was carefully polite because he distrusted his own case came long afterward and did not destroy the mood created in 1842.

Of course, the mood was reinforced by many other factors, but without doubt it was helped along by the Webster-Ashburton negotiations, and 121 years later it still persists.

Until then our contacts with the British were, as a rule, unpleasantly rough, but since then they have been the smoothest of all. Webster had much to do with establishing that mood and therein he touches your life and mine.

It was on March 7, 1850, however, that Webster probably saved the Union and ruined himself by rising to greatness. The aftermath of the Mexican War had had the usual effect of war's aftermath: It had driven the more emotional elements of the population into raving insanity. It is at such times that formerly gentle souls turn into vipers, and formerly shrewd fellows take to a braying that drowns the voice of reason.

The Mexican War had ended in 1848, and by 1850 mass hysteria had reached its height. In Congress, John C. Calhoun, for the South, and William H. Seward, for the North, were no longer arguing, they were merely screeching; and each was attended by a rabble of noisemakers whose din all but obliterated calm counsel. It was all too appallingly plain that any small spark might set off an explosion that would destroy the Union.

Then old Henry Clay, already mortally ill, summoned the last of his strength to devise the nine measures known as the Compromise of 1850 and, dying on his feet, prevented the death of his country. His success was not immediate. Because it was a genuine compromise, it was furiously attacked by both Calhoun—who was also mortally ill—and Seward, and its fate wavered in the balance week after week and month after month. So evenly matched were the contestants that eventually it became plain that all depended upon Webster, who had so far said nothing.

At last, on March 7, he rose to speak: "... not as a Massachusetts man, nor as a Northern man, but as an American ... I speak today for the preservation of the Union. 'Hear me for my cause.'" They heard. They heeded. The squabbling continued for months, but eventually the compromise was adopted and the Civil War was postponed for 10 years.

But Webster's reward was such denunciation from his own people as few American statesmen have had to endure. John Greenleaf

Webster, pursuing a runaway slave in this 1850 lampoon of his stand on the fugitive-slave law, says, "It is not every one that can perform a disagreeable duty," while the U.S. marshal following him says, "He exceeds my most sanguine expectation."

Whittier, that singularly bloodthirsty Quaker, promptly consigned him to the tomb without waiting for an attending physician's certificate:

> *from those great eyes*
> *The soul has fled:*
> *When faith is lost, when honor dies,*
> *The man is dead!*

and less melodious calumniators poured cruder vituperation on him wherever two or three of them got together.

Yet every measurement known to statistics shows clearly that from 1820 on, the South had been steadily losing and the North steadily gaining in relative strength. Nevertheless, when war did break in 1861, it took every ounce of Northern strength to win through four years of the bloodiest fighting in modern times. Few Americans realize that, in proportion to the number engaged, the American Civil War was several times as deadly as either World War I or World War II. If it had come 10 years earlier, the border states would almost certainly have gone with the South, and the outcome might have been different.

Henry Clay's Compromise of 1850 saved the Union, and Daniel Webster saved the compromise.

Still, it was not by logic that he did it. Logically, he was a Massachusetts man, a Northern man, but emotionally he was an American; and the emotional appeal, not the logic, carried the compromise. More than that, it carried Daniel Webster into the hearts of an emotional people, and there he abides. We do not believe, we cannot believe, that knowledge, logic, might, or the Devil himself can prevail against a man who loves anything strongly enough to invite his own ruin in its defense.

This characteristic of human nature is the great weakness of democracy, as has been vociferously proclaimed by every logician from Plato down. Alcibiades played upon it; so did Huey Long and Joe McCarthy and all the demagogues between. But under favorable circumstances it is also the great *strength* of democracy, as Webster, Lincoln, and the second Roosevelt instinctively recognized. It is the factor that transforms government from a science into an art—maddening the scientists, including (perhaps one should say *especially*) the social scientists, and inspiring poets and other irresponsible characters.

The obvious fact that democracy is—apparently incurably—emotional rather than logical is the despair of men who have subjected their minds to rigorous intellectual discipline, and who are therefore convinced that intellectual discipline is the only conceivable approach to truth. Thus when they perceive that the great heroes of democracy seem to bear more family likeness to Roscius, the actor, than to Aristotle, the philosopher, they tend to despair of democracy. Webster is a case in point. He was certainly a great constitutional lawyer (which is to say, a logician), but he became immortal only when he abandoned his logic and appealed to the emotions. The legal precedents he set have been largely superseded or abandoned, but the moods he established have endured for more than 100 years.

Superficially, this suggests that demagoguery casts its works in bronze, while statecraft carves in butter, which is a patent absurdity. What the rigid logicians tend to overlook is that emotionalism as a political instrument is divided into separate branches, one of which relies on love, the other on hate as its chief agency. Hope is subsidiary to love as fear is to hate. The artists, as distinguished from the scientists, in government can be classified accordingly.

There is not the slightest doubt on which side Daniel Webster's appeal to the emotions lay. He spoke as an American. He spoke for the future. He was extravagant, yes; he was turgid and bombastic, if you will. But his worst extravagance and bombast were never designed to foment hatred and fear, but always to stimulate love and pride. Therefore, the people, greatly needing both, have looked with an indulgent eye on his faults and frailties and, because he spurred them in the direction of greatness, deemed him, and still deem him, a great man.

True, the eye with which they have regarded him is not only indulgent, but a little sardonic. When his last words were reported, folklore quickly invented an explanation. People said the physician remarked to an attendant, when the end was obviously at hand, "If he is still living in an hour, give him brandy," whereupon Webster with his dying breath murmured, "I still live."

Never mind. Anyone the American people love, they laugh at. It has always been so, and it will be so until the character of the nation is changed. If Webster's spirit could return to observe what has come of the nation he saved, it is easy to believe it would be less impressed by the miraculous changes that have taken place than by the lack of any change in the common people's love of their country and pride in it. And seeing this lack of change, the disembodied spirit of the godlike Daniel could repeat, "I still live."

Gerald W. Johnson was a contributing editor to The New Republic *magazine and was the author of many books on American history.*

Volume 7
ENCYCLOPEDIC SECTION

The two-page reference guide below lists the entries by categories. The entries in this section supplement the subject matter covered in the text of this volume. A **cross-reference** (*see*) means that a separate entry appears elsewhere in this section. However, certain important persons and events mentioned here have individual entries in the Encyclopedic Section of another volume. Consult the Index in Volume 18.

AMERICAN STATESMEN

Charles Francis Adams
Edward Bates
John Bell
John Cabell Breckinridge
Preston Brooks
James Buchanan
A. P. Butler
Simon Cameron
Lewis Cass
Salmon P. Chase
Howell Cobb
John Crittenden
Davy Crockett
Jefferson Davis
Stephen A. Douglas
Edward Everett
Millard Fillmore
James Henry Hammond
Sam Houston
Joseph Lane
Abraham Lincoln
William L. Marcy
James Murray Mason
John Y. Mason
Franklin Pierce
Robert B. Rhett
William H. Seward
John Slidell
Alexander H. Stephens
Charles Sumner
Zachary Taylor
Robert A. Toombs
Isaac Toucey
Lyman Trumbull
Daniel Webster
Thurlow Weed
Gideon Welles
David Wilmot
William L. Yancey

ANTISLAVERY LEADERS

Henry Ward Beecher
John Brown
Salmon P. Chase
Frederick Douglass
Free Soil Party
Horace Greeley
Grimké sisters
John Parker Hale
Hinton Rowan Helper
William H. Seward
Harriet Beecher Stowe
Charles Sumner
Lyman Trumbull
Sojourner Truth
Harriet Tubman
Nat Turner
William Whipper

EXPLORERS AND EXPANSION

Davy Crockett
Donner Party
Stephen A. Douglas
James Gadsden

Gadsden Purchase
Sam Houston
Stephen W. Kearny
William B. Travis

FOREIGN RELATIONS

Charles Francis Adams
Alexander Baring
William L. Marcy
James Murray Mason
John Y. Mason

Ostend Manifesto
William H. Seward
John Slidell
Pierre Soulé
Treaty of Guadalupe Hidalgo
Nicholas Trist

MEXICAN WAR

James Bowie
Jefferson Davis
Alexander Doniphan
Thomas ap Catesby Jones
Stephen W. Kearny
Joseph Lane
John Y. Mason
Santa Anna

Winfield Scott
John D. Sloat
Zachary Taylor
Treaty of Guadalupe Hidalgo
Nicholas Trist
David Wilmot
Wilmot Proviso
John Ellis Wool

PRESIDENTS

James Buchanan
Millard Fillmore

Abraham Lincoln
Franklin Pierce
Zachary Taylor

THE SLAVERY ISSUE

Robert Anderson
Compromise of 1850
Confederate States of America
John Crittenden
Crittenden Compromise
Jefferson Davis
Thomas Roderick Dew
Stephen A. Douglas
Dred Scott case
Freeport Doctrine

Free Soil Party
Fugitive Slave Law
Harpers Ferry
Kansas-Nebraska Act
Lincoln-Douglas debates
Mason and Dixon Line
Nat Turner's Rebellion
"peculiar institution"
Robert B. Rhett
slavery
underground railroad

THOUGHT AND CULTURE

Charles Francis Adams
James Gordon Bennett
Thomas Roderick Dew
Dixie
Daniel Decatur Emmett
Horace Greeley
Hinton Rowan Helper

Know-Nothing Party
Herman Melville
Edgar Allan Poe
John Roebling
Harriet Beecher Stowe
Uncle Tom's Cabin
James Walker

A

ADAMS, Charles Francis (1807–1886). As United States minister to Britain (1861–1868), Adams was one of the men most responsible for keeping Britain from declaring war against the United States during the Civil War. In 1861, when two Confederate emissaries, **James M. Mason** and **John Slidell** (*see both*), were removed by a Union naval captain from the British ship *Trent*, in violation of neutrality laws, a clamor for war spread through Britain. Realizing the gravity of the situation, Adams advised Secretary of State **William Seward** (*see*) to release the two men. Seward did so, and the danger of war was removed. Adams' earlier years had been devoted to literary activity. He wrote political articles for pamphlets and magazines and in the early 1840s edited the letters of his grandmother, Abigail Adams (1744–1818). Opposed to slavery, he was editor of the Boston *Whig* from 1846 to 1848. He was engrossed for six years (1850–1856) in preparing for publication the ten-volume *Works of John Adams,* which included the political writings of his grandfather, President John Adams (1735–1826). With the breakup of the Whig Party, Adams joined the Republicans and in 1858 was elected to Congress, where he served until sent to Britain as minister three years later. He traveled again to Europe in 1871 as one of the arbitrators of the *Alabama* claims dispute. He helped to settle claims brought by the United States against Britain for the losses inflicted by the Confederate cruiser *Alabama* and other ships built or armed in England during the Civil War in violation of neutrality laws. From 1874 to 1877, Adams was

Charles Francis Adams

occupied editing the memoirs of his father, President John Quincy Adams (1767–1848), which were published in 12 volumes.

ANDERSON, Robert (1805–1871). Anderson was the Union commander at Fort Sumter in 1861 when the shot that began the Civil War was fired. Although forced to surrender the fort, he returned to it four years later to personally reestablish Union control. A native of Kentucky, Anderson had graduated from West Point in 1825. He served under General **Winfield Scott** (*see*) in the Mexican War and was wounded in 1847 at the Battle of Molino Del Rey. In 1860, Anderson, then a major, was put in command of troops in Charleston, South Carolina. Because of the increasing talk of secession by South Carolina leaders following Lincoln's election in November, 1860, Anderson had the guns at Fort Moultrie in Charleston Harbor spiked and moved his 68 troops to Fort Sumter on December 26. This fort, which was also situated in the harbor, was inaccessible by land. When a Union

ship bringing reinforcements was fired upon by Confederate shore batteries in January, 1861, Anderson refrained from returning the fire. On April 11, Confederate General **P. G. T. Beauregard** (*see*) ordered Anderson to evacuate Fort Sumter. Running short of supplies and hoping to avoid conflict, Anderson agreed to do so by April 15, provided new supplies had not yet arrived. His offer was rejected by Confederate forces, which began shelling the fort on April 12, 1861. After 34 hours, Anderson surrendered and the Union flag over the fort was lowered. Ill health forced Anderson to retire in 1863. However, he returned to Fort Sumter on April 14, 1865, with the original flag and raised it again over the fort.

B

BARING, Alexander (1774–1848). Baring, who was the First Baron Ashburton, negotiated with **Daniel Webster** (*see*) the Webster-Ashburton Treaty between the United States and Britain in 1842. This treaty settled several boundary disputes between the two nations, including the present border between Maine and Canada. Born into a prominent family of bankers, Lord Ashburton was a noted financier and statesman. He represented his family's firm in America, was a Member of Parliament (1806–1835), and served as president of the Board of Trade and as Master of the Mint (1834). Ashburton was appointed in the spring of 1842 as a commissioner to Washington, D.C., to settle the boundary questions, which had remained unresolved since the end of the Revolutionary War. Negotiations between him and Webster began in June, and the treaty was signed on August 9. Later, both governments answered opposition to the treaty by exhibiting conflicting maps to prove they had not made too many concessions.

BATES, Edward (1793–1869). A noted Missouri lawyer, Bates, who was Attorney General (1861–1864) for most of the Civil War, was the first person from the area west of the Mississippi River to hold a cabinet position. Born in Virginia, Bates moved to Missouri in 1814, where he subsequently practiced law and held several public offices, including a term in the House of Representatives (1827–1829). A leader of the Whig Party in Missouri and an opponent of slavery, Bates aligned himself with the Republicans in the mid-1850s. He unsuccessfully sought the Republican nomination for President in 1860. His high standing in that party led **Abraham Lincoln** (*see*) to appoint Bates to his cabinet the next year. At his suggestion, the navy began equipping a fleet on the Mississippi River. Bates resigned in November, 1864, because he believed that three other members of Lincoln's cabinet—**Salmon P. Chase, William H. Seward** (*see both*), and Edwin M. Stanton (1814–1869)—had abused their authority. Bates returned to Missouri, where he opposed the antislavery Radical Republicans who had gained control of the state government. He considered their disregard for law and civil rights dangerous and revolutionary.

BEAUREGARD, Pierre Gustave Toutant (1818–1893). P. G. T. Beauregard was the Confederate general whose order to fire upon Fort Sumter in 1861 began the Civil War. Born on his father's plantation in Louisiana, Beau-

P. G. T. Beauregard

regard graduated from West Point in 1838 and joined the corps of engineers. Assigned to General **Winfield Scott** (*see*) in the Mexican War, he distinguished himself during the siege of Veracruz and also helped to plan the capture of Mexico City. In 1861, Beauregard was appointed superintendent of West Point, but he served only five days, resigning when Louisiana seceded from the Union. Beauregard applied for a commission to **Jefferson Davis** (*see*), who appointed him a brigadier general in the Confederate Army and put him in command of forces in the Charleston, South Carolina, area. On April 12, 1861, Beauregard directed the bombardment of Fort Sumter. After Major **Robert Anderson** (*see*) surrendered the fort, Beauregard was transferred to Virginia and was a hero at the First Battle of Bull Run near Manassas, Virginia, in July, 1861. He was promoted to the rank of full general and took over command of the Confederate forces at the Battle of Shiloh on April 6 and 7, 1862, when General Albert Sidney Johnston (1803–1862) was killed. Beauregard was relieved of his command in the summer of 1862 because of ill health and differences with Davis over how to conduct the war. He later served in

the defense of the South Carolina and Georgia coasts. At the close of the war, Beauregard was with the Confederate Army in the Carolinas that was among the last to surrender. He later became president of a New Orleans railroad and adjutant general of Louisiana. Beauregard and Davis continued their feud in several books published after the war.

BEECHER, Henry Ward (1813–1887). As one of the most popular and influential preachers of the 19th century, Beecher used the pulpit to advocate such reforms as abolition and women's suffrage. Born in Litchfield, Connecticut, the son of Lyman Beecher (1775–1863), a famous Congregational minister, young Beecher was expected to follow his father's profession. Although he experienced religious doubts after graduating from Amherst College in 1834, Beecher obediently entered Lane Theological Seminary in Cincinnati. Ordained a Presbyterian—he later became a Congregationalist—Beecher preached in Indiana from 1837 to 1847. By 1847, his reputation as an orator had become widespread, and he accepted a pastorate at the Plymouth Congregational Church in Brooklyn, New York, where he served until his death 40 years later. Beecher's magnetic personality attracted huge audiences, sometimes as many as 2,500 persons in a week. His sermons, which were also printed and distributed, dealt with political and social as well as religious subjects. He zealously denounced slavery and believed that if slavery was confined to the Southern states, it would vanish of its own accord. Opposed to the **Compromise of 1850** and the **Fugitive Slave Law** (*see both*), Beecher condoned the use of force to make Kansas a free state. In 1856, Beecher, representing his congregation, purchased some rifles—nicknamed Beecher's Bibles—for abolitionist forces in the Kansas-Nebraska border dispute. During the Civil War, Beecher went on a lecture tour to England to enlist sympathy for the Union

This sculpture, presumably of Henry Ward Beecher, was carved in 1840.

cause. Afterward, he crusaded in journals, churches, and lecture halls for women's rights and came out in support of the evolution theories of naturalist Charles Darwin (1809–1882), explaining that they were consistent with a belief in God.

BELL, John (1797–1869). Bell, who was a prominent Tennessee lawyer and statesman, was the Constitutional Union Party's candidate in the election of 1860. Carrying only Tennessee, Kentucky, and Virginia, he split the Democratic Party vote and thus contributed to the victory of **Abraham Lincoln** (*see*). Born near Nashville, Bell became a lawyer and entered state politics before serving in the House of Representatives (1827–1841), where he ultimately became the leader of the Tennessee Whigs. In 1841, he was Secretary of War for several weeks during the brief administration of William Henry Harrison (1773–1841), who died one month after taking office. As Senator from Tennessee (1847–1859), Bell—who was a conservative and a slave owner—emerged as an opponent of both Southern and Northern extremists. He firmly opposed secession and believed wholeheartedly in the preservation of the Union. These views led the moderate Constitutional Union Party, which was formed in late 1859, to nominate him, with **Edward Everett** (*see*) as his running mate. The party's ideals were expressed in its platform, "The Constitution of the country, the Union of the States and the enforcement of the laws." After the Civil War began and Tennessee seceded, Bell accepted his state's decision to join the Confederacy. When Union troops invaded his state, he left there to go farther into the South and spent the war lamenting the conflict.

BENNETT, James Gordon (1795–1872). Bennett, who founded the New York *Herald* in 1835, was the first editor to provide brief editorials on all political parties, to give accounts of Wall Street financial activities, and to report crimes and scandals in a sensational manner. He was also the first to use foreign correspondents to gather the news and the telegraph to relay it. Born in Scotland, Bennett immigrated to Nova Scotia in 1819 and four years later settled permanently in New York. He made a name for himself as a journalist (1827–1832) while on the staff of the New York *Enquirer* and its successor, the *Morning Courier and New York Enquirer.* When that paper switched its allegiance from the Democrats to the Whigs, Bennett resigned, determined to found his own newspaper. The result was the *Herald,* which sold for 1¢ a copy. It was an immediate success, largely because, as one critic put it, it was filled "with vulgarity, vituperation, and scandal." However, the paper's news coverage was excellent. For the most part the *Herald* supported the Democratic Party. Before the outbreak of the Civil War it favored secession, but it supported the Union after hostilities began in 1861. When Bennett turned over the editorship to his son, James Gordon Bennett (1841–1918), in 1867, the *Herald* had the largest circulation of any New York paper, reaching about 90,000 people daily.

BOWIE, James (1796?–1836). A well-known frontiersman and the reputed designer of the famed bowie knife, Bowie was one of the more than 180 defenders who died at the Alamo in 1836. Bowie was born in Georgia and moved to Louisiana in 1802. According to tradition, he and two brothers, Rezin and John Bowie, sold slaves smuggled into Texas and Louisiana by the pirate Jean Laffite (1780?–1826?). Bowie moved again in 1828, settling in Texas, where he prospected for a lost mine and speculated in land. Two years later, he became a Mexican citizen, though he played a leading role as a colonel in the revolutionary movement against the Mexican government. He participated in the campaign of 1835 that drove the Mexican army out of Texas. When **Santa Anna** (*see*) led his army back into Texas, Bowie, Colonel **William B. Travis** (*see*), and about 150 men retreated from San Antonio and took their stand at the Alamo, a mission-fort, where they received some reinforcements. When the Alamo fell on March 6, 1836, Bowie, lying on his cot ill with pneumonia, was slain.

BRECKINRIDGE, John Cabell (1821–1875). A leading Southern statesman and at one time Vice-President of the United States, Breckinridge was a Southern general and also the Confederate Secretary of War during the Civil War. Born and educated in Kentucky, Breckinridge, a lawyer, served in the Mexican War as a major. Afterward, he was elected to the state legislature (1849–1851) and in 1851 to the House of Representatives. He remained in the House until 1856, when he was chosen by the Democratic Party as the running mate for its Presidential candidate, **James Buchanan** (*see*). When Buchanan entered the White House in 1857, Breckinridge, as Vice-President, became president of the Senate. Although a supporter of slavery, he presided over the Senate with impartiality during the difficult period preceding the Civil War. After being defeated in 1860 as the Presidential nominee of proslavery Southern Democrats, Breckinridge entered the United States Senate the following year. When Kentucky decided in September, 1861, to stay in the Union, Breckinridge resigned and joined the Confederate Army, saying, "I exchange with proud satisfaction a term of six years in the Senate of the United States for the musket of a soldier." The Senate later declared him a traitor and formally expelled him. As a general during the Civil War, Breckinridge participated in, among others, the Battles of Shiloh, Murfreesboro, Chickamauga, and New Market. Early in 1865, **Jefferson Davis** (*see*) appointed him Secretary of War. After the dissolution of the Confederate cabinet with the end of the war that same year, Breckinridge fled by horse to Florida and from there sailed to Cuba and then England. He was later granted permission by the federal government to return to America. He came back to Kentucky in 1868 and resumed his law practice.

BROOKS, Preston Smith (1819–1857). A South Carolina Representative and a proponent of slavery, Brooks is perhaps best remembered for his violent attack upon abolitionist Senator **Charles Sumner** (*see*) of Massachusetts on May 22, 1856. Brooks—angered when Sumner insulted his uncle, Senator **A. P. Butler** (*see*)—beat up Sumner (*see pp. 558–559*) so seriously that it was more than three years before Sumner returned to the Senate. Born on a plantation in South Carolina, Brooks was elected to the state legislature in 1844, five years after graduating from college. He was a captain during the Mexican War and was first elected to the House of Representatives in 1852. When Sumner, who opposed the **Kansas-Nebraska Act** (*see*), gave a speech in which he characterized Butler as a Don Quixote paying vows to "the harlot, Slavery," Brooks was incensed. Two days later he stormed into the Senate chamber and knocked Sumner unconscious with a walking cane. Northerners condemned Brooks' action, but Southern states passed resolutions praising him and sent Brooks gold-headed canes to commemorate the incident. Although a vote taken in the House to expel Brooks failed to achieve the necessary two-thirds majority, Brooks resigned. His constituents, however, promptly reelected him to the House by a unanimous vote. Less than a year after his attack on Sumner, Brooks died.

BROWN, John (1800–1859). The fiery, controversial abolitionist who led the raid on the federal arsenal at **Harpers Ferry** (*see*) was either hailed as a martyr or denounced as a fanatic. Born in Connecticut into a family with a record of mental illness, Brown was taught to abhor slavery by his father, who was an abolitionist. After receiving a scanty education, he tried and failed at various businesses and often moved his wife and children from state to state. About 1825, he settled in Pennsylvania, where his barn served as a station on the **underground railroad** (*see*). Later, he organized the League of Gileadites at Springfield, Massachusetts, which taught blacks how to defend themselves and also protect fugitive slaves. In 1849, he moved to North Elba, New York, a black community. From the time he was about 50 years old, Brown became increasingly preoccupied with the idea of using force to end slavery. Five of his sons migrated to Kansas in 1855 to fight to have slavery outlawed in the new territory (*see* **Kansas-Nebraska Act**). Brown followed shortly thereafter, and he soon became the leader of a small guerrilla band that terrorized proslavery settlers. On May 24, 1856, his men ruthlessly murdered five of them at Pottawatomie, Kansas, an act that Brown said God had commanded him to perform. Hoping to stir up a general slave insurrection, Brown made plans in 1858 for a new state in the mountains of Maryland and Virginia. It was to be a refuge for escaped slaves, and from it he planned to launch a general slave revolt. Brown set up a base of operations the following year at a farm near Harpers Ferry in the present state of West Virginia. There he collected arms and recruited followers. On Octo-

John Brown

LIBRARY OF CONGRESS

ber 16, Brown, with about 20 men, took over the United States arsenal at Harpers Ferry. Instead of then escaping into the mountains with the weapons he had seized, Brown and his men remained in the town. Meanwhile, the state militia sealed off all possible escape routes. On October 18, Union Army Colonel Robert E. Lee (1807–1870) and a detachment of marines captured Brown and killed about 10 of his men, including one of his sons.

Brown was tried for murder and treason at Charlestown, Virginia, and sentenced to die. He refused to have his lawyers plead insanity to change his sentence. He was hanged on December 2, 1859. The popular Union marching song *John Brown's Body* has been erroneously associated with Brown. The words were actually written by members of a Massachusetts infantry company to spoof one of their sergeants who was also named John Brown.

BUCHANAN, James (1791–1868). As the 15th President of the United States, in the years just prior to the Civil War, Buchanan attempted to preserve the Union at all costs, but he ended up alienating both the North and the South. Born near Mercersburg, Pennsylvania, the son of Irish immigrants, Buchanan graduated from Dickinson College in 1809, studied law, and in 1812 began a legal career. Although a Federalist, he supported the War of 1812 against Britain and afterward served in the state legislature (1814–1816). He gave up politics in 1816, intending to get married. However, he quarreled with his fiancée, and when she died shortly afterward, Buchanan decided to devote the rest of his life to politics and never did marry. He was elected to the House of Representatives in 1821. During his 10 years in the House, he abandoned the Federalist Party and became a Democrat. In 1831, he was appointed minister to Russia by Andrew Jackson (1767–1845) and after two years abroad returned home and was elected a Senator from Pennsylvania (1834–1845). Buchanan emerged as a leader of the Democratic Party. He opposed slavery on moral and political grounds. However, he declared that because the Con-

James Buchanan

NEW-YORK HISTORICAL SOCIETY

stitution protected slavery wherever it already existed, the government was obligated to protect the interests of slave owners. He denounced abolitionists as instigators of dissension. As Secretary of State (1845–1849) under James K. Polk (1795–1849), Buchanan helped formulate an expansionist foreign policy. He managed the annexation of Texas in 1845, secured Oregon for the United States in 1846, and drafted the **Treaty of Guadalupe Hidalgo** (*see*), which ended the Mexican War in 1848. Appointed minister to Britain (1853–1856) by President **Franklin Pierce** (*see*), Buchanan earned the hatred of abolitionists by helping to draft the **Ostend Manifesto** (*see*), which urged the United States to either purchase or seize Cuba from Spain. Cuba would then presumably have become a slave state. Backed by Northerners willing to make concessions to the South, as well as by most Southerners, Buchanan won the Democratic nomination for President in 1856 and was elected by a narrow margin. He tried to create in his administration a "sacred balance" between proslavery and antislavery interests. However, his cabinet members were also indecisive and showed the same lack of leadership as their President. Buchanan favored states' rights over the powers of the federal government and opposed Congressional interference with slavery in the territories where it already existed. Faced with impending disunion, Buchanan made unsuccessful efforts to mediate between the North and the South. After **Abraham Lincoln** (*see*) was elected President in November, 1860, Buchanan entered his most crucial period in office. South Carolina seceded. Buchanan admitted that the state had no right to do this, but he helplessly noted that the federal government could use force only to collect taxes or protect United States property and that it had no authority to suppress this kind of rebellion. Refusing to protect federal forts in South Carolina, Buchanan promised the state that no hostilities would occur so long as negotiations continued. However, when Major **Robert Anderson** (*see*) moved his troops to Fort Sumter, the South accused Buchanan of breaking his word, and shortly after his term expired and Lincoln took office, the fort was shelled. During the Civil War, Buchanan supported the Union.

BUTLER, Andrew Pickens (1796–1857). A Senator (1846–1857) from South Carolina, A. P. Butler was the center of a dispute between his nephew, Representative **Preston Brooks,** and Massachusetts Senator **Charles Sumner** (*see both*). Sumner, who had insulted Butler in a speech, was attacked by Brooks in the Senate on May 22, 1856, and seriously injured. Butler, who was born in South Carolina, became a lawyer in 1819 and soon built up a successful practice. First elected to the state legislature in 1824, he advocated that South Carolina nullify the tariff passed by Congress

in 1828. Butler held several positions as a judge prior to his election to the Senate in 1846. A friend of John C. Calhoun (1782–1850), who was the senior Senator from South Carolina, Butler himself became an influential champion of the interests of slaveholders. Sumner's speech insulting Butler was delivered in response to a speech Butler had made in favor of the **Kansas-Nebraska Act** (*see*). In ill health, Butler died a year after his nephew's attack on Sumner.

C

CAMERON, Simon (1799–1889). A politician whose name was often tinged by corruption, Cameron served briefly as Secretary of War (1861–1862) under **Abraham Lincoln** (*see*) and later became the boss of Pennsylvania's Republican Party. Cameron amassed a small fortune by investments in railroads, newspapers, and industries, and he exerted a powerful political influence in his state before being appointed in 1838 to adjust some claims of the Winnebago Indians. In the process of making the settlements, Cameron used his own bank to make the settlement payments, thus increasing his personal wealth. This earned him the nickname The Great Winnebago Chief. He subsequently served (1845–1849 and 1857–1861) in the Senate and in 1856 aligned himself with the Republicans. Emerging as a possible Presidential candidate at the party's 1860 convention, Cameron threw his support to Lincoln in return for a place in the cabinet if Lincoln was elected. Although Lincoln had been unaware of the bargain his backers had made he honored it by appointing Cameron Secretary of War in March, 1861. However,

Cameron's favoritism in awarding army appointments and granting contracts forced Lincoln to remove him from the cabinet. He did so by naming Cameron as minister to Russia in January, 1862. Disgruntled, Cameron resigned the following November after brief service in St. Petersburg and later was elected to the Senate (1867–1877). In the meantime, he had gained complete control of the state Republican machine, which subsequently became so powerful that it dominated Pennsylvania politics until the 1930s.

CASS, Lewis (1782–1866). A proponent of expansion in the West, Cass was the unsuccessful Democratic candidate for President in 1848. He lost to **Zachary Taylor** (*see*). Cass, a lawyer and veteran of the War of 1812, served as governor of the Michigan Territory (1813–1831) and negotiated 22 treaties with the Indians for the sale of land to the United States. In 1831, President Andrew Jackson (1767–1845) appointed him Secretary of War. Cass left the cabinet in 1836 to become minister to France, where be persuaded that nation not to ratify a five-party treaty granting the right to search American vessels. He resigned when the Webster-Ashburton Treaty was signed in 1842 because it allowed Britain to search United States ships. He next served as Senator from Michigan (1845–1857) and was appointed in 1857 as Secretary of State under President **James Buchanan** (*see*). He resigned three years later when Buchanan decided against defending the forts in Charleston, South Carolina, in the face of growing Southern hostility.

CHASE, Salmon P. (1808–1873). Chase, a founder of both the Liberty Party in the 1840s and the **Free Soil Party** (*see*) in 1848, was one of the most vigorous opponents of slavery before the Civil War. In 1864, he was appointed Chief Justice of the Supreme Court by President **Abraham Lincoln** (*see*). Chase was born in New Hampshire. After graduation from Dartmouth College in 1826, he became a lawyer in Cincinnati, where he was a leader in the antislavery movement, often defending in court fugitive slaves who had been captured. As a Senator from Ohio (1849–1855), he opposed the **Compromise of 1850** and the **Kansas-Nebraska Act** (*see both*). After helping to found the Republican Party in Ohio, Chase was elected governor of the state (1855–1859). He was elected to the Senate again in 1860 but served only two days in March, 1861, resigning to be Secretary of the Treasury (1861–1864) in Lincoln's cabinet. As such, he oversaw the financing of the Civil War and instituted a national banking system in 1863. Chase resigned from the cabinet in 1864 after a dispute with Lincoln over political appointments, but friendly relations were soon resumed and Chase was elevated to the Supreme Court that same year. As Chief Justice, Chase achieved a notable record, especially in his impartial handling of the impeachment of President Andrew Johnson (1808–1875) in 1868, over which he presided. He also reorganized the federal court system in the South and presided over the treason trial of **Jefferson Davis** (*see*) in 1867, favoring Davis' pardon.

COBB, Howell (1815–1868). A prominent national political figure, Cobb resigned as Secretary of the Treasury after the election of **Abraham Lincoln** (*see*) and played a

Howell Cobb

crucial role in the secession of the Southern states. Born into a family of wealthy Georgia planters, he studied law and was elected to the House of Representatives in 1842, serving until 1851, the last two years as Speaker. Cobb's constituents were primarily small farmers who, having no economic stake in slavery, were pro-Union. In 1851, Cobb was elected governor of Georgia on a platform supporting the **Compromise of 1850** (*see*) and the Union. Cobb returned to the House in 1855, and the following year he supported **James Buchanan** (*see*) in the Presidential election. Cobb was subsequently named Secretary of the Treasury by Buchanan in 1857. As the sectional dispute over slavery grew more bitter, Cobb lost confidence in the Union. With Lincoln's election in 1860, he resigned from the cabinet and went back to Georgia to press for its secession from the Union. He was elected chairman of the convention that organized the **Confederate States of America** (*see*) in 1861 and later joined the Confederate Army, forming his own regiment.

He rose to the rank of major general before the war was over, serving chiefly in Virginia and his own state.

COMPROMISE OF 1850. The growing sectional differences between the North and the South over states' rights and the extension of slavery were temporarily settled by this compromise, which was proposed by Henry Clay (1777–1852). The controversy had been building up ever since the Missouri Compromise of 1820 had set a line running along the southern border of Missouri, to determine the status of new states entering the Union from territory in the Louisiana Purchase. States above the line were free; below, slave. The South was pleased when proposals for admitting Texas were made in 1845, because most of Texas lay within slave territory. However, the following year, Northern Congressmen introduced the **Wilmot Proviso** (*see*) in an attempt to ban slavery from Texas, and political parties split along sectional lines. When, on January 16, 1850, a bill was introduced in Congress to organize the territories of California, Utah, and New Mexico, the South insisted once more that the Missouri Compromise be extended to the Pacific and asserted that any attempt by the federal government to outlaw slavery from these territories would be unconstitutional. A few days later, President **Zachary Taylor** (*see*) recommended that California, which had drafted a constitution prohibiting slavery, be admitted as a state. Southern leaders, afraid that the addition of a free state without the admission of a slave state would upset the balance in the Senate, again began talking about seceding from the Union. In an effort to maintain national unity, Clay proposed that California be admitted as a free state, that the Utah and New Mexico territories be allowed to practice slavery, and that the slave trade—but not slavery—be abolished from the District of Columbia. In addition, he urged the enactment of a stiffer **Fugitive Slave Law** (*see*) so that runaway slaves would be returned to their owners, and he also proposed that Texas be compensated for abandoning land claims in New Mexico. Following stormy debates, Clay's proposals, in the form of five separate bills, were enacted in August and September of 1850. These became known as the Compromise of 1850.

When this $100 bill was issued in 1864, Confederate money was almost worthless.

CONFEDERATE STATES OF AMERICA.

On February 4, 1861, delegates from six Southern states that had seceded from the Union—Alabama, Florida, Georgia, Louisiana, Mississippi, and South Carolina—met in Montgomery, Alabama, to form a separate government. **Howell Cobb** (*see*) of Georgia was chosen president of the convention. By February 8, a provisional constitution was adopted, and on the next day **Jefferson Davis** (*see*) of Mississippi and **Alexander Stephens** (*see*) of Georgia were chosen President and Vice-President, respectively, of the Confederate States of America. The constitution was based on the federal Constitution, but the guarantee of states' rights was made explicit. The Confederate constitution said that each of the Confederate states would act "in its sovereign and independent capacity." Other measures, such as protective tariffs and appropriations for internal improvements, were expressly forbidden. Most other appropriations required a two-thirds majority for approval. The limited power of the central government was to create problems for the Confederacy in its execution of the war. The President could serve for only one six-year term and thus was limited in the authority he could exercise. Member states were represented in both chambers of the Confederate Congress, but their representatives often disagreed with one another at the expense of a concerted defense of the Confederacy. Judicial power was vested in a supreme court, but this provision was never implemented, and it was left to individual state courts to interpret the constitution. The right of ownership of slaves was protected, but the further importation of slaves from abroad was prohibited. Congress was also given the right to ban the importation of slaves from any state not in the Confederacy, a provision that was designed to convince two slave states—Maryland and Virginia—to join the Confederacy. Voters confirmed the decisions made by the delegates in Montgomery in an election held in November, 1861. Texas became the seventh state to join the Confederacy in March, 1861, and four more states—Arkansas, North Carolina, Tennessee, and Virginia—joined shortly after President **Abraham Lincoln** (*see*) asked for volunteers to fight the Confederacy on April 15, 1861. Maryland, however, stayed in the Union. The Confederate flag bore 13 stars. The additional two were for governments-in-exile from the border states of Kentucky and Missouri. Following the outbreak of the Civil War in the spring of 1861, the capital of the Confederacy was moved from Montgomery to Richmond, Virginia, where it remained until the last days of the war.

CRITTENDEN, John Jordan

(1787–1863). A Kentucky Senator, Crittenden tried to prevent civil war from breaking out between the North and the South by proposing a series of measures known as the **Crittenden Compromise** (*see*). After his effort failed, Crittenden was instrumental in keeping Kentucky in the Union during the war that followed, but his two sons joined opposing armies. Crittenden was first appointed to fill a vacancy in the Senate in 1817. After two years, he returned to Kentucky and became well-known as a criminal lawyer and was active in state politics. He returned to the Senate in 1835, serving until 1841, and was later reelected twice (1843–1849 and 1855–1861). He served under three Presidents— William Henry Harrison (1773–1841), John Tyler (1790–1862), and **Millard Fillmore** (*see*)—as Attorney General (1841 and 1850–1853) and in between was elected governor (1848–1850) of Kentucky. During his last term in the Senate in 1860, Crittenden proposed his compromise, believing, he said, that the dissolution of the Union would be the "consummation of the greatest evil that can befall us." It centered on restoring and extending the boundary line between free and slave states first established by the Missouri Compromise of 1820. However, President **Abraham Lincoln** (*see*) refused to go along with any extension of slavery and fought to defeat the compromise. After his proposal failed, Crittenden went back to Kentucky to urge his state to remain in the Union, and he later represented it in the House (1861–1863). During the Civil War, his son George Bibb Crittenden (1812–1880) was a Confederate officer, while another son, Thomas Leonidas Crittenden (1819–1893), was a major general in the Union Army.

CRITTENDEN COMPROMISE.

This compromise was an effort to settle the increasing disputes between backers of slavery and abolitionists over new states joining the Union. At the heart of the compromise—proposed by Senator **John Crittenden** (*see*) of Kentucky on December 18, 1860—was a proposal to restore the boundary line between slave and free states established by the Missouri Compromise of 1820. The line, which had been invalidated by the **Kansas-Nebraska Act** (*see*) of 1854, would have been extended to new territories in the West. North of it, slavery would be prohibited. South of the line, slavery would be permitted and protected by the federal government. In addition, the compromise included five other

amendments and four resolutions. These would have denied to Congress the power to abolish slavery in slaveholding states or to rescind any laws, such as the **Fugitive Slave Law** (*see*), that protected slave owners. However, President **Abraham Lincoln** (*see*) refused to support any compromise that provided for the extension of slavery, and the proposal was defeated in Congress.

CROCKETT, David ("Davy")

(1786–1836). Crockett's colorful exploits as a frontiersman, politician, and soldier have made him a national folk hero in modern times. He was born to a poor family in the backwoods region of what is now Tennessee. He found book learning difficult and attended school for only six months, but he became adept at the skills

Treed by a bear, Davy Crockett—so the tale goes—fought back with a knife.

needed to survive in a frontier wilderness. Crockett served as a scout under Andrew Jackson (1767–1845) in the Creek War (1813–1814). Although illiterate, he was elected to the Tennessee legislature (1821–1823) and later represented the state (1827–1831 and 1833–1835) in Congress. During his years in Washington, D.C., he continued to wear his frontiersman's costume, achieved renown for his ribald humor, and was popularly referred to as the coonskin Congressman. Crockett opposed Jackson's policy of forcing Indians off their lands into reservations, and in 1835 he joined the Whig Party. This cost him reelection in his Tennessee district, which supported Jackson, a Democrat. Crockett then became interested in the cause of Texas independence and in 1836 journeyed there to aid **Sam Houston** (*see*) in fighting the Mexicans. He died in the fall of the Alamo on March 6, 1836 (*see pp. 562–563*).

D

DAVIS, Jefferson (1808–1889).

The man who was President of the **Confederate States of America** (*see*) was a reluctant secessionist who had previously served as a United States Senator and Secretary of War. Davis, a native of Kentucky, was raised in Mississippi. He was educated at West Point, from which he graduated in 1828. Davis then served seven years on the Western frontier. In 1835, he married Sarah Knox Taylor (1814–1835), the daughter of **Zachary Taylor** (*see*). Three months after the marriage, Sarah died of malaria and Davis went into seclusion on his plantation. Davis owned slaves, some of whom he taught to read and write. He allowed them to conduct their own trials and to decide upon punishments. Davis believed that slavery was a temporary necessity to maintain the cotton economy of the South and that blacks had to be educated before they could become citizens. In 1845, Davis married Varina Howell (1826–1906) and ran for the House of Representatives. After serving one year, he resigned to fight in the Mexican War. Davis' regiment prevented defeat at the Battle of Buena Vista in February, 1847, though Davis was wounded. Returning home, he entered the Senate in 1847 and became a leading proponent of states' rights. He resigned in 1851 to run for governor of Mississippi. After losing a close election, Davis returned to his plantation. In 1853, President **Franklin Pierce** (see) selected Davis as his Secretary of War. Davis improved West Point, raised the pay of the military, increased the size of the armed forces, introduced new weapons, and built up coastal defenses. He was also responsible for commissioning surveys of three railroad routes to the West. In 1857, Davis returned to the Senate. Although he believed that a state had the right to secede, he was reluctant to see individual states leave the Union because he was certain it would lead to war. After South Carolina's secession in December, 1860, Davis tried to achieve a compromise acceptable to both sides. He also urged President **James Buchanan** (see) to withdraw federal troops from Fort Sumter, in Charleston Harbor, to avoid a conflict. In January, 1861, when Mississippi seceded, Davis delivered an emotional farewell address to the Senate, in which he pleaded with the North to allow secession to occur peaceably. Mississippi commissioned Davis a major general, but before he could

assume those duties, he was chosen provisional President of the Confederacy by the Southern states meeting in Montgomery, Alabama. Davis was undoubtedly the foremost statesman in the Confederacy, and it was hoped that his moderate views would encourage the secession of other states. Davis still hoped to avoid armed conflict, but he believed he could not allow the Union forces to resupply Fort Sumter and thus control the South's major port. Early in April, 1861, Davis authorized General **P. G. T. Beauregard** (see) to order the evacuation of Fort Sumter, and if the order was refused, to fire upon it. On April 12, after the fort's commander, **Robert Anderson** (see), refused to surrender, Beauregard's forces began shelling the fort. The tragic war that Davis had struggled to avoid had begun. (*Entry continues in Volume 8.*)

Jefferson Davis

DEW, Thomas Roderick (1802–1846). A Virginia-born educator and writer, Dew published a pro-slavery essay in 1832 that was extremely influential in the South. He believed that slavery had made possible the cultural development of the ancient world and that civilization was the result of the thoughts of a few and the work of many. Dew graduated from the College of William and Mary in Virginia in 1820 and in 1827 was appointed to teach political law there. The courses he taught included "History, Metaphysics, Natural and National Law, Government and Political Economy." From 1836 until his death, he was president of the college. In his *Lectures on the Restrictive System* (1829), Dew advocated free trade and opposed protectionism on the ground that it would lead to disunity between the industrial North and the agricultural South. Some historians believe that this work subsequently influenced Congress to lower tariffs. However, Dew's most influential work was his defense of slavery, *A Review of the Debate in the Virginia Legislature of 1831 and 1832,* which was published in 1832. This pamphlet was widely popularized after it was reprinted with the title "Professor Dew on Slavery" in *The Pro-Slavery Argument* (1852), a collection of Southern essays.

DIXIE. *See* **Emmett, Daniel.**

DONIPHAN, Alexander William (1808–1887). During the Mexican War, Doniphan commanded a famous expeditionary force that captured the city of Chihuahua and contributed substantially to the success of the American campaign in northern Mexico. Born in Kentucky, Doniphan moved to Missouri in 1830, where he subsequently became a prominent lawyer and politician. In May, 1846, Doniphan organized the 1st Regiment of Missouri Mounted Volunteers. The following month, his regiment joined the army of **Stephen W. Kearny** (*see*) at Fort Leavenworth, Kansas, and together the two units marched to Santa Fe, New Mexico, which they occupied with no opposition on August 18. There the two forces split up. Kearny's army headed for California, while Doniphan remained in New Mexico and made a peace treaty with the Navaho Indians, who had been harassing settlers. In December, 1846, he led his regiment toward Chihuahua, where it was supposed to support General **John Wool** (*see*). Doniphan's troops defeated the Mexicans at the Battle of El Brazito on December 25 and occupied El Paso two days later. Following another victory at Sacramento on February 28, 1847, Doniphan seized control of Chihuahua on the following day. When Wool did not appear as planned, Doniphan continued on to Saltillo, which he reached in late May. He then followed the Rio Grande to the Gulf of Mexico and sailed for New Orleans. His force had covered 3,600 miles by land and 2,000 miles by water in less than a year under adverse conditions and with few losses. Doniphan later resumed his legal career in Missouri and participated in local politics. Before the outbreak of the Civil War, he opposed secession and advocated that his state remain neutral. After the commencement of hostilities, Doniphan was made a major general in the Missouri state guard, but he resigned after only two weeks because his two sons were killed in an accident and his wife became seriously ill. He then practiced law in Richmond, Missouri, until his death.

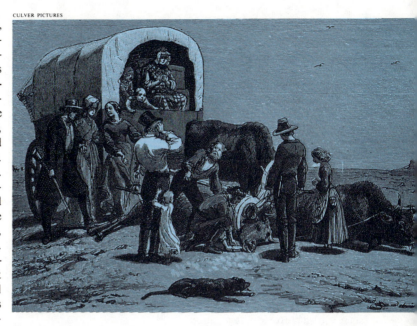

The Donner Party began losing oxen and horses on the arid salt flats of Utah.

DONNER PARTY. The terrible hardships endured by the Donner Party—a group of settlers bound for California during the winter of 1846–1847—have become one of the legends of the Western frontier. The party was organized by the Donner and Reed families of Sangamon County, Illinois. On April 16, 1846, the caravan of wagons and oxen started on its journey, heading west toward California. Other settlers joined on the way, and by the time the party reached present-day Utah it included 87 persons, nearly half of whom were children. In order to save time—it was already late summer—the leaders of the party decided to shorten the journey by taking an untried route south of the Great Salt Lake. The horrors of the expedition began with the six-day crossing of the salt flats south of the lake, where many of the oxen and horses died. The settlers continued on through the early autumn, harassed by Indians and torn by internal quar-

rels. By early November, they were struggling up through the foothills of the Sierra Nevada. High in the mountains they were caught in a blinding eight-day snowstorm. They built huts and waited, in two squalid camps five miles apart, for rescue parties. On February 4, a small relief expedition drawn from several California settlements set out through shoulder-deep snow and two weeks later arrived at the campsites with a small amount of food. The rescuers found that some of the settlers had survived by eating those who had died. Other rescue parties subsequently got through, and the last members of the Donner Party were brought to safety on April 25, 1847. Of the original 87, only 47 were left. The site where they had been snowbound is now called Donner Pass.

DOUGLASS, Frederick (1817?–1895). A former slave who became a famous speaker and writer, Douglass dedicated his life to winning freedom and equality for blacks. Born in Tuckahoe, Maryland, he was the son of an unidentified white man and a slave, Harriet Bailey, who named him Frederick Augustus Washington Bailey. During childhood, Frederick was treated cruelly, overworked, and neglected. However, the wife of his owner taught him to read and write, and in 1838 he succeeded in escaping to New York City, where he changed his name to Frederick Douglass to avoid detection. He then went to New Bedford, Massachusetts, where he worked as a day laborer. He met abolitionists, and at their request, spoke before the Massachusetts Anti-Slavery Society in 1841. His speech was so moving that the society hired him to lecture to other groups. For the next four years, Douglass toured the Northeast, delivering lectures with such eloquence that people wondered if he had in fact been a slave. To convince them, Douglass published in 1845 the first version of his autobiography, *Narrative of the Life of Frederick Douglass*. The book—a classic portrayal of the indignities suffered by slaves—contained so many specific details that he was advised to burn it, lest he be identified by his owner. Instead, Douglass spent the next two years in Britain, and with the money he earned from his speaking engagements abroad, returned to America in 1847 and purchased his freedom. That same year, he founded a newspaper for blacks, the *North Star*, in Rochester, New York. During his 17 years as editor of the weekly, Douglass agitated for full citizenship for blacks through legal and peaceful channels. He helped **Harriet Beecher Stowe** (*see*) establish a technical school to train black youths. Douglas disapproved of the violence used by his friend **John Brown** (*see*) in the raid on **Harpers Ferry** (*see*) in 1859. Although he had not been involved in the raid, Douglass was accused of complicity by Virginia authorities and fled to Canada and from there to Britain. He stayed abroad for six months. When the Civil War broke out, Douglass urged blacks to fight for the North. He himself organized two black regiments and often advised **Abraham Lincoln** (*see*) on black problems. After the war, Douglass encouraged freedmen to vote and demand their civil rights. In later life, Douglass held several government posts, including federal marshal for the District of Columbia (1877–1881) and United States minister to Haiti (1889–1891).

DOUGLAS, Stephen A. (1813–1861). This Illinois Senator sponsored the **Kansas-Nebraska Act** (*see*) and debated **Abraham Lincoln** (*see*) in a series of campaign speeches known as the **Lincoln-Douglas debates** (*see*). Douglas, a native of New York, went west as a young man to establish himself. Arriving in Illinois in 1833 with only 75¢ in his pocket, he taught school during the day and studied law at night. Douglas was licensed to practice law the following year and soon earned a reputation for being the "best lawyer in a bad case." By the age of 28 he was appointed a judge of the Illinois supreme court. Nicknamed the Little Giant because of his short but stocky figure and aggressive self-confidence, Douglas threw himself into Illinois politics with great energy. He rose to power in that state's Democratic Party. After two unsuccessful attempts, Douglas was elected to the House of Representatives in 1843. He resigned his seat four years later to enter the Senate, where he served until his death in 1861. As chairman of the Com-

Stephen A. Douglas

mittee on Territories, a position he held in both the House and Senate, Douglas urged the development and expansion of the West. He supported the annexations of Texas and Oregon and favored the Mexican War (1846–1848). To hasten the development of new territory, he opposed the **Wilmot Proviso** (*see*), which would have excluded slavery in any territory gained as a result of the Mexican War. Douglas believed that settlers should decide for themselves whether to permit slavery in a territory. Accordingly, he supported the **Compromise of 1850** (*see*), which applied his concept of popular sovereignty to New Mexico and Utah, and introduced the Kansas-Nebraska Act, which allowed both Kansas and Nebraska to determine for themselves the question of slavery. When President **James Buchanan** (*see*) recommended a Congressional bill admitting Kansas under the Lecompton Constitution, Douglas was so angered that he quit the Democratic Party. When Douglas ran for reelection to the Senate in 1858, he was challenged by Lincoln. Douglas won after engaging in seven debates with Lincoln, but he had come out in support of the extension of slavery in the campaign and so ruined his chances for higher office. In 1860, he ran for President on an independent ticket, thereby splitting the Democratic vote and assuring Lincoln's election. With the outbreak of the Civil War, Douglas fully supported Lincoln's Republican administration. While making a tour of the Northwest in an effort to gain support for the North, he was stricken with typhoid fever and died in Chicago.

DRED SCOTT CASE. In 1857, the Supreme Court handed down one of the most controversial rulings in its history in the case of *Dred Scott vs. Sandford.* Dred Scott (1795?–1858) was a slave then living in Missouri. He had first sued for his freedom in state courts in 1846 (*see pp. 559–560*). Scott contended that because he had previously resided with his master both in the free state of Illinois and in the Wisconsin Territory, where slavery had been prohibited by the Missouri Compromise of 1820, he was automatically a freeman. When the Missouri supreme court ruled against him, Scott, encouraged by abolitionists, appealed to the United States Supreme Court. It ruled that because Scott was a slave, he was not a citizen and therefore was not entitled to sue in a federal court. The ruling further said that because he was a resident of the slaveholding state of Missouri, he was not affected by the laws of a free state such as Illinois. The Court also held unconstitutional the Missouri Compromise, which prohibited slave ownership in Northern territories. This was done on the ground that taking a slave to free soil did not liberate him, because under the Bill of Rights citizens could not be deprived of their property (in this case, slaves) without due process of law. Slaves, the Court said, were "chattel property . . . so far inferior that they have no rights which the white man is bound to respect." The ruling in the Dred Scott case, the first in more than 50 years to declare an act of Congress unconstitutional, intensified bitterness between the North and the South.

E

EMMETT, Daniel Decatur (1815–1904). Composer of *Dixie,* the favorite marching song of the Confederate Army and now considered the "anthem" of the South, Emmett was a songwriter and minstrel-show singer. Born in Ohio, Emmett joined the circus as a young man and in 1842 organized one of the first companies of blackface minstrels, calling them the Virginia Minstrels. The troupe first performed at the Bowery Amphitheatre in New York. After playing in Boston, it traveled to Britain, where Emmett stayed until 1844. He composed *Dixie* in 1859 after hearing touring minstrels complain about the cold climate of the North. Bryant's Minstrels sang it for the first time as a "walk-around"—a curtain-call parade by the performers—in Mechanics Hall, New York. Instantly popular, *Dixie* was first used as a Confederate song at the inauguration of **Jefferson Davis** (*see*) as President of the Confederacy in 1861.

EVERETT, Edward (1794–1865). A prominent political figure and statesman from Massachusetts, Everett was the Constitutional Union Party's candidate for Vice-President in the election of 1860. Along with his running mate, **John Bell** (*see*), he pledged himself to "the Constitution of the country, the Union of the States, and the enforcement of the laws." Everett had graduated from Harvard College in 1811. He became a Unitarian minister, and after studying in Europe, he taught Greek literature (1819–1825) at Harvard. He subsequently was elected to the House of Representatives (1825–1835), was governor of Massachusetts (1836–1840), and served as ambassador to Britain (1841–1845). He was chosen president of Harvard in 1846 but resigned three years later because he did not like the administrative duties. Everett served briefly as Secretary of State at the close of the administration of President **Millard Fillmore** (*see*) and was elected to the Senate in 1853. Everett was mainly concerned with the preservation of the Union and believed that abolitionist agitation would lead to its dissolution. Because this compromising attitude toward slavery ran counter to the antislavery stand dominant in Massachusetts, he resigned from the Senate in 1854. He later devoted himself wholeheartedly to the Union cause during the Civil War and lectured widely in support of Lincoln's administration.

F

FILLMORE, Millard (1800–1874). Fillmore, the 13th President of the United States, succeeded **Zachary Taylor** (*see*), who died in office on July 9, 1850. He served as Chief Executive for only two years. A moderate on the slavery issue, Fillmore attempted to reconcile the North and the South and supported the **Compromise of 1850** (*see*). However, his backing of the **Fugitive Slave Law**

Millard Fillmore

(*see*) alienated Northern abolitionists, who united behind **Winfield Scott** (*see*) and denied Fillmore the Whig nomination for President in 1852. Fillmore was born in Locke, New York, the son of a poor farmer. He received little schooling in his youth but at the age of 18 began the study of law under a judge in Cayuga County, New York. He was admitted to the New York bar in 1823 and later practiced law in Buffalo. Fillmore's first political experience was in the state legislature (1829–1831). An associate of political boss **Thurlow Weed** (*see*), Fillmore served four terms in the House of Representatives (1833–1835 and 1837–1843). At first a member of the Anti-Masonic Party, he became a Whig in 1834. In the House, Fillmore, an advocate of protection for American industry, helped draft the tariff of 1842. He was defeated in the race for governor of New York in 1844, but with the backing of Henry Clay (1777–1852) and **Daniel Webster** (*see*), secured the Whig Vice-Presidential nomination in 1848. As President, Fillmore reorganized the postal system and sent Commodore **Matthew C. Perry** (*see*) to open trade with Japan. In 1856, Fillmore was the Presidential candidate of the

Know-Nothing Party (*see*) but was soundly defeated. He then returned to Buffalo, where he practiced law until his death on March 8, 1874.

FREEPORT DOCTRINE. In one of the important **Lincoln-Douglas debates** (*see*) held during the Illinois Senatorial campaign of 1858, **Stephen A. Douglas** (*see*) formulated what came to be known as the Freeport Doctrine. On August 27, during the debate at Freeport, in northwestern Illinois, **Abraham Lincoln** (*see*) asked Douglas to clarify his position on popular sovereignty. Did the settlers of a federal territory, Lincoln asked, have the right to prohibit slaveholding, or must they abide by the Supreme Court decision in the **Dred Scott case** (*see*), which guaranteed slave-owning citizens protection for their "property [slaves]"? Douglas answered that territorial inhabitants could decide the issue of slavery for themselves. This argument, which asserted that popular sovereignty took precedence over the Dred Scott decision, was soon labeled the Freeport Doctrine. Douglas' stand, popular in Illinois, helped return him to the Senate in 1858 but deprived him of Southern support in the Presidential election two years later.

FREE SOIL PARTY. The Free Soil Party, founded at Buffalo, New York, on August 9, 1848, advocated "no more slave states and no more slave territory." The party also favored the awarding of free land to homesteaders on the frontier. It came into being as a cooperative effort by opponents of slavery in both the Whig and the Democratic Parties, together with advocates of land re-

form and members of the older Liberty Party, which had experienced little success. At its first convention, the Free Soil Party nominated former President Martin Van Buren (1782–1862) and **Charles F. Adams** (*see*) to run as President and Vice-President, respectively. Campaigning for "Free Soil, Free Speech, Free Labor and Free Men," the party polled more than 290,000 votes in 1848. It won enough votes in New York State to prevent Democrat **Lewis Cass** from defeating **Zachary Taylor** (*see both*). About a dozen Free Soil candidates won election to Congress that same year. In 1852, however, the party's Presidential nominee, **John P. Hale** (*see*), made a weak showing at the polls, and two years later the Free Soilers disbanded and many joined the new Republican Party.

FUGITIVE SLAVE LAW. The Fugitive Slave Law was one of five bills that collectively are known as the **Compromise of 1850** (*see*). It was designed to eliminate the aid being given runaway slaves by members of the **underground railroad** (*see*). The law, which placed all fugitive-slave cases under federal jurisdiction, provided for special commissioners authorized to issue both warrants for the arrest of runaway slaves and certificates for their return to their owners. A master had only to present a commissioner with an affidavit of ownership to reclaim a runaway slave. If the affidavit was accepted and the slave was returned to his master, the commissioner received a $10 fee. If rejected, he got $5. The act also provided heavy penalties for its evasion. Citizens concealing a runaway slave or preventing his arrest or return were liable to a $1,000 fine, up to six months' imprisonment, and civil damages of

$1,000 for each slave that escaped as a result of their aid. Marshals and deputies who refused to issue warrants for the arrest of fugitive slaves were likewise liable for a $1,000 fine. They could also be sued for the value of any slave who escaped their custody. In practice, however, the Fugitive Slave Law stimulated abolitionists to help slaves to escape bondage. Thousands of fugitives fled from the free states into Canada to avoid capture, still assisted by the underground railroad. The law so infuriated abolitionist **Harriet Beecher Stowe** (*see*) that she wrote *Uncle Tom's Cabin,* which was published in book form in 1852.

G

GADSDEN, James (1788–1858). A Southern railroad promoter, Gadsden acquired in 1853 the territory from Mexico known as the **Gadsden Purchase** (*see*), which he hoped would enable the South to construct a railroad to the Pacific coast. Born in Charleston, South Carolina, Gadsden graduated from Yale in 1806. He served in the army for 10 years and afterward became a planter in the Florida Territory. In 1839, he returned to Charleston and the following year became president of a railroad that in 1842 was incorporated as the South Carolina Railroad Company. For the next several years, Gadsden tried unsuccessfully to unite the small independent railroads of the South into one continuous line that would extend to the Pacific. He hoped thereby to make the West economically dependent on the South, rather than on the Northeast. In 1853, he decided that a line along the Gila River, in the present states of New Mexico and Arizona, would be the most feasible route. Because this land belonged to Mexico, Gadsden exerted political pressure to get himself appointed minister to Mexico so that he could negotiate its purchase. Seeing that the Mexican dictator, **Santa Anna** (*see*), was in financial trouble, Gadsden attempted to acquire a larger portion of Mexican territory than he had intended. However, the Senate would only agree to buying enough land for the construction of a railroad. Gadsden died before the railroad was built.

GADSDEN PURCHASE. The present southern boundary of the United States was determined in 1853 by the purchase from Mexico of a narrow, 29,000-square-mile strip of land known as the Gadsden Purchase. The motive behind the purchase was Congress' search for a feasible transcontinental railway route to the Pacific coast. The South, whose rivalry with the Northeast was accentuated by the **Compromise of 1850** (*see*), hoped that the proposed rail line would run through the Deep South and then continue west by skirting the Rocky Mountains to cross a region then belonging to Mexico. **Jefferson Davis** (*see*), a radical proponent of Southern interests and Secretary of War under President **Franklin Pierce** (*see*), persuaded Pierce to send **James Gadsden** (*see*), a South Carolina railroad promoter, to Mexico to buy the land required for the railway route. Gadsden was named the minister to Mexico and in 1853 negotiated the purchase with Mexico's president, **Santa Anna** (*see*), for $15,000,000. However, both the area involved and the purchase price were reduced by the Senate before it ratified the agreement in 1854. The Senate limited the area to only what was needed to build the railroad. However, construction on the Southern Pacific Railroad, which ran through the land, was not begun until after the Civil War. The territory finally covered was bounded on the east by the Rio Grande, on the north by the Gila River, and on the south by the Colorado River—thus establishing the southern boundaries of the present states of Arizona and New Mexico. The price was set at $10,000,000.

GREELEY, Horace (1811–1872). Greeley, who popularized such slogans as "Go West, young man," was one of America's greatest newspaper editors. The founder of the New York *Tribune,* he exerted a significant influence on American politics for 30 years through his vigorous editorials. Born in New Hampshire, Greeley worked as an editor's apprentice on a Vermont weekly, and when it closed down in 1830, he moved to New York City and became a printer's apprentice. He started the *New Yorker,* a nonpartisan weekly news and cultural journal in 1834. Greeley contributed to and edited various Whig periodicals before he founded the *Tribune* in April, 1841. This newspaper, which was merged with the *New Yorker* the following September, was noted for its accurate news reporting, high intellectual standards, distinguished staff, and good taste—it barred scandal and sensationalism from its pages. By 1846, it was one of New York's most respected papers. Its most outstanding feature was Greeley's editorials. During the *Tribune's* first decade, Greeley attacked the Mexican War, business monopolies, and slavery. He championed democratic causes such as the formation of labor unions, women's rights, temperance, and the agrarian movement, which advocated the free distribution of land to settlers. He frequently advised young men to seek their fortunes in the West, and although he did not coin the phrase, "Go West, young man," he made it a popular slogan. During the 1850s, Greeley's antislavery stand gained in intensity, and he wrote some of his most eloquent editorials against the controversial **Kansas-Nebraska Act** (*see*) of 1854. Although he had endorsed the nomination of **Abraham Lincoln** (*see*) for the Presidency in May, 1860, Greeley criticized some of Lincoln's war policies. He disapproved of the President's conciliatory attitude to the border slave states, saying he abhorred the idea of any "complicity in slavery extension." He also urged the early emancipation of the slaves. After the war, Greely campaigned for full equality for blacks and favored a general amnesty to end the sectional antagonism that still existed between the North and the South. A candidate for the Presidency on the Liberal Republican ticket in the election of 1872, Greeley was soundly trounced by Ulysses S. Grant (1822–1885). The defeat, which came a few days

This drawing of abolitionist Horace Greeley was entitled "Man of Wrath."

after his wife's death, and his subsequent discovery that he had virtually lost editorial command of the *Tribune,* led to a complete nervous breakdown. Greeley died insane a few weeks later.

GRIMKÉ SISTERS. Sarah Moore Grimké (1792–1873) and her sister, Angelina (1805–1879), repudiated their Southern heritage and crusaded for the abolition of slavery. Born in Charleston, South

Sarah and Angelina Grimké

Carolina, to an aristocratic planter family, both girls at an early age revolted against their background. In about 1819, Sarah became influenced by some Philadelphia Quakers and joined that sect. Angelina, the more independent of the two, followed her sister to Philadelphia but soon became disillusioned with the Quakers' rigid beliefs and their noncommittal attitude toward slavery. Much to the disapproval of Sarah and the Quakers, Angelina in 1835 wrote William Lloyd Garrison (1805–1879), one of the nation's leading abolitionists, to express her views on the slave question. The following year, Angelina wrote the eloquent *Appeal to the Christian Women of the South,* urging them to "overthrow this horrible system of oppression." The pamphlet was popular among abolitionists, but in Charleston it was burned and Angelina was threatened with jail if she ever returned there. At

this time, Sarah abandoned the Quaker sect to help Angelina lecture to groups of women for the American Anti-Slavery Society. In 1838, the sisters persuaded their mother to give them the slaves belonging to them as part of their inheritance. They immediately freed them. The Grimkés began speaking before audiences of both men and women. They met with so much prejudice against women's speaking in public that the sisters took up the cause of women's rights as well as slavery and enlisted the support of many abolitionists for a second reform movement. In 1838, Angelina married the abolitionist Theodore Weld (1803–1895), and both she and Sarah aided him in setting up a school in New Jersey devoted to liberal ideas.

H

HALE, John Parker (1806–1873). A radical abolitionist, Hale was the Presidential candidate of the **Free Soil Party** (*see*) in the election of 1852, which was won by **Franklin Pierce** (*see*). Born in New Hampshire, Hale was a successful lawyer and politician in his state before serving (1834–1841) as United States District Attorney. He was elected as a Democrat to the House of Representatives in 1843 but was expelled from that party in February, 1845, because of his antislavery views. Running as an independent, Hale was elected a Senator two years later and for his next six years in the Senate was an outspoken critic of slavery. He ran for President in 1852 on the Free Soil platform of "no more slave states and no more slave territory." Although defeated in the national contest, Hale was reelected to the Senate in 1855 and soon became a leading member of the newly formed Republican Party. He served as chairman of the Committee on Naval Affairs during the Civil War, but his acceptance of a fee from a contractor convicted of fraud by the government cost him the support of the Republican Party when his Senate term expired in 1864. Hale later served (1865–1869) as minister to Spain.

HAMMOND, James Henry (1807–1864). A Senator from South Carolina, Hammond was one of the earliest to advocate that the South secede from the Union and set up its own government. He bitterly resented Northern attempts to dominate the South and boasted in the Senate on March 4, 1858, "You dare not make war on cotton—no power on earth dares make war upon it. Cotton is king." A graduate of South Carolina College (1825), Hammond afterward studied law and became a successful attorney in Columbia. In 1830, he began publishing a newspaper, the *Southern Times,* to spread his political ideas. An ardent defender of states' rights, he believed that slavery was "the cornerstone of our Republican edifice." He opposed tariffs and urged Southern states as a group to sever ties with the federal government. Hammond served in the House of Representatives (1835–1836), was governor of South Carolina (1842–1844), and was elected to the Senate in 1857. After 1855, he devoted much of his time to overseeing his plantation on Beach Island in the Savannah River, where he owned thousands of acres of land and more than 300 slaves. Although highly critical of **Jefferson Davis** (*see*) and the Confederate Congress, Hammond supported the South during the Civil War.

HARPERS FERRY. This village, strategically situated at the meeting point of the Potomac and Shenandoah Rivers in present-day West Virginia, was captured briefly in an 1859 raid by the abolitionist **John Brown** (*see*) and later was fought over by Union and Confederate forces. The town lay near the Shenandoah Valley and was a gateway to the slaveholding lands of the South. It was named after Robert Harper, who had established a ferry crossing at the site in 1734. A federal arsenal was built there in 1796, and during the first half of the 19th century, the town was important because of its proximity to iron-ore deposits and because of the availability of waterpower for industry. Brown seized Harpers Ferry on October 16, 1859, because he wanted the weapons in the arsenal to arm a widespread slave rebellion that he was planning. However, he and his men were captured at the town's engine house two days later. Nine battles were subsequently fought in the vicinity of Harpers Ferry during the Civil War. For the most part, the town remained in Union control.

HELPER, Hinton Rowan (1829–1909). Although a lifelong enemy of black people, Helper wrote a widely read, bitter attack on slavery which intensified the ill feeling between the North and the South that helped to bring on the Civil War. The book, *The Impending Crisis of the South, and How to Meet It,* was a result of Helper's personal bitterness as a youth on a poor North Carolina farm. He blamed the plight of poor white farmers in the South on their inability to compete with the "free" labor provided by slaves. When he published *The Impending Crisis* in 1857, it caused

a furor that surpassed even the emotional agitation created by **Harriet Beecher Stowe** (*see*) in her *Uncle Tom's Cabin.* Helper's book was banned in the South, while abolitionist Republicans in the North circulated more than 100,-000 copies during the campaign of 1860. Helper moved to New York and later wrote such violently racist books as *Negroes in Negroland* (1868). President **Abraham Lincoln** (*see*) appointed him United States consul at Buenos Aires, Argentina, in 1861. Helper served in that post until 1866 and then tried for many years, without success, to promote a railroad from Hudson Bay, Canada, to the Strait of Magellan in South America. In 1909, protesting that "There is no justice in this world," he killed himself.

HOUSTON, Samuel ("Sam") (1793–1863). This famous soldier and statesman became the first president of the Republic of Texas after defeating the Mexicans at the Battle of San Jacinto in April, 1836, nine years before Texas became a state. Houston, who was born in Virginia, moved with his family to the Tennessee frontier about 1807 and subsequently lived among the Cherokee Indians for three years. He won acclaim for his bravery while serving under Andrew Jackson (1767–1845) in the campaign against the Creek Indians in 1814. Four years later, Houston returned to Tennessee, where, despite his scanty formal education, he became a lawyer. His height—he was six feet two inches tall—his good looks, and his fiery and dramatic personality made him a popular figure among the frontier population, and he was elected to several minor public offices before serving (1823–1827) in the House of Representatives.

In 1827, he was elected governor of Tennessee but resigned two years later after his bride deserted him. Houston settled among the Cherokees in what is now Oklahoma, where he established himself as a trader at a government Indian post and began to drink heavily. He was adopted by the Cherokees, who called him The Raven. In 1835, Houston moved to Texas, and the following year he was elected commander in chief of the army raised by Texas settlers to throw off Mexican control. Houston became a hero on April 21, 1836, when he defeated and captured the Mexican general **Santa Anna** (*see*) in a surprise attack at San Jacinto (*see pp. 564–565*). He served two terms (1836–1838 and 1841–1844) as president of the Republic of Texas, and after Texas was admitted to the Union in 1845, he was one of the first two Senators from Texas (1846–1859) in Congress. Houston lost his bid for reelection to the Senate in 1859 because of his uncompromising Union stand. He had been the only Southern Senator to vote for all the measures of the **Compromise of 1850** (*see*) and had opposed the **Kansas-Nebraska Act** (*see*) of 1854. Houston summed up his position by saying, "I am

for the Union without any 'if' in the case; and my motto is, it shall be preserved!" However, he was still popular enough to win election as governor of his state that same year. He was deposed in March, 1861, after the people of Texas, acting against his advice, voted to secede from the Union. Houston refused to take an oath of allegiance to the Confederacy and was denounced as a "hoary haired traitor." He then retired to his farm at Huntsville.

J

JONES, Thomas ap Catesby (1790?–1858). In 1842, four years before the Mexican War broke out, Jones, who commanded the American squadron in the Pacific Ocean, captured Monterey, California, acting on the false assumption that hostilities had begun between the United States and Mexico. Jones, a native of Virginia, was of British and Welsh descent. The *ap* in his name was derived from the Welsh prefix meaning "son of." He entered the navy as a midshipman in 1805 and subsequently helped suppress the slave trade, piracy, and smuggling in the Gulf of Mexico. On

December 14, 1814, during the War of 1812 with Britain, Jones made a desperate but unsuccessful attempt to prevent the fleet that was transporting the British army to New Orleans from crossing Lake Borne. In 1826, he went to the Hawaiian Islands, where he protected American interests in the face of an attempt to make the islands a British dependency. In the fall of 1842, Jones was stationed off Peru, where he heard rumors that war had broken out with Mexico. Believing that a British fleet intended to capture California, he did not wait for instructions but rushed northward with two ships. On October 20, Jones seized the public buildings at Monterey and raised the American flag. The following day he was informed that America and Mexico were not at war. Jones apologized profusely for the fiasco, and the American government disavowed the act. He was relieved of his command but regained it two years later.

K

KANSAS–NEBRASKA ACT. The territories of Kansas and Nebraska were created in 1854 by an act of Congress that proved to be one of the most far-reaching laws in United States history. Sponsored by Illinois Senator **Stephen A. Douglas** (*see*), the Kansas-Nebraska Act provided that settlers in these new territories would decide for themselves whether to permit slavery within their borders. The act specifically repealed the Missouri Compromise of 1820, which had prohibited slavery in the western United States north of latitude 36° 30', a line that ran along the southern border of Missouri. Many Americans had believed the

Although wounded, Sam Houston directed Texans to victory at San Jacinto in 1836.

N. ORR N.Y.

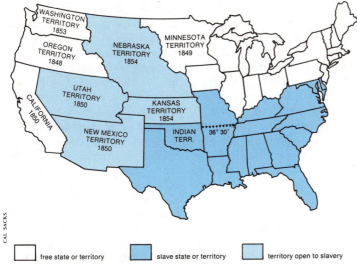

WASHINGTON TERRITORY 1853

OREGON TERRITORY 1848

NEBRASKA TERRITORY 1854

MINNESOTA TERRITORY 1849

UTAH TERRITORY 1850

CALIFORNIA 1850

KANSAS TERRITORY 1854

NEW MEXICO TERRITORY 1850

INDIAN TERR.

36° 30'

CAL. SACKS

☐ free state or territory   ■ slave state or territory   ☐ territory open to slavery

The Kansas-Nebraska Act of 1854 failed to settle the controversy over slavery.

issue of slavery was settled by the **Compromise of 1850** (*see*). However, when Douglas introduced the Kansas-Nebraska bill in January, 1854, the bitter issue flared anew. Most Northerners denounced the legislation as inviting the spread of slavery throughout the West, while Southerners demanded that new states and territories have a choice on the matter of slavery. Several months of fierce debate in Congress followed before the bill became law on May 30. Soon after its passage, "Bleeding Kansas" became a battleground between proslavery and antislavery settlers. Opponents of the act joined forces to form the Republican Party. The Kansas-Nebraska Act intensified antagonism between the North and the South and helped to hasten the Civil War.

KEARNY, Stephen W. (1794–1848). Kearny, a general who had joined the army before the War of 1812, commanded 1,600 troops that set out from Fort Leavenworth, Kansas, in 1846 to conquer New Mexico and California. His men were able to occupy Santa Fe without

opposition, and from August to September Kearny acted as military governor of New Mexico. At the end of September, he resumed his march west, this time to wrest California from the hands of the Mexicans. He took with him 300 dragoons for the nearly 900-mile journey to San Diego. On the way, Kearny met the famous scout Kit Carson (1809–1868), who told him that California had been taken by the Americans. Upon learning this, Kearny sent 200 men back to Santa Fe and proceeded on with the remaining 100. Although defeated by Mexican forces at the Battle of San Pascual, east of San Diego, on December 6, 1846, Kearny, who was wounded in the battle, finally reached San Diego with about 70 men. He then occupied Los Angeles and acted as governor of California during the spring of 1847. Kearny later became civil governor of Veracruz.

KNOW-NOTHING PARTY. The Know-Nothing Party opposed Roman Catholicism and the admission of immigrants to the United States. The party grew out of the

Order of the Star Spangled Banner, a secret society founded in New York in 1849. Its official title was the American Party. The name Know-Nothing came into popular use because party members, when questioned about their organization, always claimed to "know nothing." In the 1840s and 1850s, large numbers of immigrants, especially Irish Catholics, poured into the United States. This angered many native Americans, who feared that the new arrivals would get their jobs and also exert influence in politics. The Know-Nothings demanded that immigration be limited, that citizenship be granted only after 21 years of residence in the country, and that aliens and Roman Catholics be excluded from public office. In 1856, the Know-Nothings put forward former President **Millard Fillmore** (*see*) as their Presidential candidate, but he carried only one state. Although the party did not achieve national power, it was often politically successful on local and state levels. The Know-Nothing Party broke up in the late 1850s over the slavery issue, but later organizations, such as the Ku Klux Klan, revived its basic program.

L

LANE, Joseph (1801–1881). Lane was a prominent Oregon politician who ran for Vice-President on the pro-Southern Democratic ticket headed by **John C. Breckinridge** (*see*) in 1860. A native of North Carolina, Lane became a prosperous farmer in Indiana and served several terms in that state's legislature. At the outbreak of the Mexican War in 1846, he resigned from the state senate to join the army. Lane commanded a brigade at the Battle of Buena Vista in February, 1847, under General **Zachary Taylor** (*see*) and was brevetted a major general for his bravery in the action. In 1848, he was named governor of the Oregon Territory. Lane resigned this position in 1850 to become the territorial delegate to the House of Representatives. He served in that capacity until 1859, when he became one of the first two Senators (1859–1861) from the state of Oregon. In 1860, Lane was nominated for Vice-President by the Southern Democrats. With his defeat in the election, Lane returned to his home in Oregon and retired from politics.

LINCOLN, Abraham (1809–1865). The 16th President of the United States was a backwoods farm boy and prairie lawyer before he rose to national prominence and led the Union through the bloody and tragic Civil War (1861–1865). Considered one of the nation's greatest Chief Executives, Lincoln became known as the Great Emancipator, although he was never considered an abolitionist and was more concerned with preserving the Union than abolishing slavery. The son of Thomas Lincoln (1778–1851) and Nancy Hanks Lincoln (1784?–1818), Abe Lincoln was born in a log cabin near Hodgenville, Kentucky. The family moved to Indiana in 1816. Although his formal education was scanty, Lincoln read extensively and studied on his own. In 1831, Lincoln settled in New Salem, near Springfield, Illinois. By this time, he was a strong, lanky young man six feet four inches tall. During the next six years, he held various jobs, working as a storekeeper, mill manager, rail-splitter (*see p. 608*), postmaster, and surveyor. He also served as a captain in the

Black Hawk War in 1832. Lincoln was very popular in New Salem because of his storytelling ability, honesty, sincerity, and physical strength. As a Whig member (1834–1841) of the Illinois legislature, Lincoln was neither a supporter of slavery nor an abolitionist. In 1837, he moved to Springfield, where he established a law practice, and five years later he married Mary Todd (1818–1882). Lincoln served one term (1847–1849) in the House of Representatives, during which he maintained his conservative attitude toward slavery. He advocated its gradual abolition in the city of Washington, D.C., if the citizens of the capital approved, and he believed that slaveholders should be compensated for their losses. Lincoln subsequently became a leading lawyer in Illinois, arguing cases before state and federal courts. He reemerged on the political scene in 1854 when he attacked **Stephen A. Douglas** (*see*), the Democratic Senator from Illinois, and the **Kansas-Nebraska Act** (*see*), which Douglas sponsored. The act permitted the extension of slavery into new territories. Taking a firmer stand against slavery than he had ever done, Lincoln aligned himself with the recently formed Republican Party. When that party nominated him as a Senator from Illinois, he made an eloquent acceptance speech on June 16, 1858. It contained the prophetic statement, "A house divided against itself cannot stand." The following July, Lincoln challenged his Democratic opponent, Douglas, to a series of debates. In the ensuing **Lincoln-Douglas debates** (*see*), Lincoln stressed his moderate attitude toward slavery by opposing the extension of the institution and by again disclaiming any abolitionist aims. Douglas

won the election, but Lincoln had gained national prominence and became the Republican Party's Presidential candidate for the election of 1860. After a campaign in which he stayed in Springfield and avoided political speeches, Lincoln the following November defeated three opponents—**John C. Breckinridge, John Bell** (*see both*), and Douglas. He did not receive a majority of the popular vote but won enough electoral votes to be elected. There were 10 Southern states where he did not receive a single popular vote. By the time Lincoln took office four months later on March 4, 1861, seven Southern states had seceded from the Union and formed the **Confederate States of America** (*see*). In his inaugural address, Lincoln promised not to interfere with slavery in Southern states or slaveholding territories, but he also declared that he would "hold, occupy, and possess" all federal property within the Confederacy and that the Union would not countenance secession. When the Civil War broke out with the Confederate shelling of Fort Sumter on April 12, 1861, Lincoln turned to the prosecution of the war, hoping to end it swiftly. (*Entry continues in Volume 8.*)

LINCOLN–DOUGLAS DEBATES. Seven three-hour debates between **Abraham Lincoln** and **Stephen A. Douglas** (*see both*) were the most colorful events of the Illinois Senatorial race of 1858 and marked Lincoln's emergence as a national figure. Lincoln, the Republican candidate who was contesting Douglas' reelection, challenged the Little Giant, as Douglas was known, to the debates, which were held from August 21 to October 15 in seven Illinois towns: Ottawa, Freeport,

Jonesboro, Charleston, Galesburg, Quincy, and Alton. When the two men met, they differed in appearance as well as opinion. Lincoln, lean and angular, was a full foot taller than the broadly built Douglas, and he wore baggy clothes in marked contrast to Douglas' ruffled shirt and well-tailored suit. The subject of the debates was slavery. In his opening speech at Ottawa, Douglas attacked Lincoln for having said earlier that summer that "A house divided against itself cannot stand." Douglas charged that Lincoln's views would result in equality for blacks and integration. Lincoln answered that he had no intention of interfering with slavery in states where it already existed but that he opposed its extension. The most notable debate was the one held at Freeport on August 27. Lincoln asked Douglas how he could reconcile the Supreme Court decision in the **Dred Scott case** (*see*), upholding the right of slaveholders to take their slaves into the territories, with the concept of popular sovereignty—that is, the right of citizens to decide their own laws. Douglas replied that the right to admit or bar slavery in a new state existed in spite of the Court's decision, "for the reason that slavery cannot exist a day or an hour anywhere, unless it is supported by local police regulations." This view, that people of a territory could exclude slavery by lawful means before statehood, became known as the **Freeport Doctrine** (*see*). The argument swung the Senatorial election for Douglas in Illinois but provoked such criticism in the South that Douglas, deprived of Southern political backing, lost the Presidential election of 1860 to Lincoln. Afterward, Douglas gave his full support to Lincoln.

M

MARCY, William L. (1786–1857). Marcy, who coined the term *spoils system,* was a leading political figure and statesman of the first half of the 19th century. In 1832, while defending the practice of rewarding the party faithful with government jobs and favors, he maintained that there is "nothing wrong in the rule that to the victor belong the spoils." Marcy was born in Massachusetts. He graduated from Brown University in 1808 and practiced law in Troy, New York. He soon allied himself with one of the most powerful state political machines in the nation, which was popularly known as the Albany Regency. Marcy was appointed associate justice of the New York supreme court in 1829. He resigned that post two years later when elected to the United States Senate. He left the Senate the following year to serve three terms (1833–1839) as governor of New York. Marcy was Secretary of War (1845–1849) in the administration of James K. Polk (1795–1849) and Secretary of State (1853–1857) under **Franklin Pierce** (*see*). A skilled mediator, Marcy handled many important diplomatic negotiations, including the **Gadsden Purchase** (*see*) of 1853, but he was less successful in dealing with the scandal surrounding the **Ostend Manifesto** (*see*) in the mid-1850s. He left office in March, 1857, and died a few months later.

MASON, James Murray (1798–1871). As a United States Senator from Virginia, Mason drafted the **Fugitive Slave Law** (*see*) of 1850. He later served as a Confederate diplomat and was one of two Southern ministers involved in

James Murray Mason

the *Trent* Affair in 1861. A native of Georgetown, Virginia (now part of Washington, D.C.), Mason graduated from the University of Pennsylvania in 1818. Long active in Virginia politics, he was elected to the House of Representatives in 1837 and served one term. Eight years later, he returned to Washington as a Senator. In 1850, hoping to suppress the growing incidence of runaway slaves, he drafted the controversial Fugitive Slave Law. A strong proponent of states' rights, Mason believed that war between the North and South was inevitable after **Abraham Lincoln** (*see*) was elected President in 1860. He left the Senate early the next spring, and the Confederate government appointed him a commissioner to Britain that same year. He and **John Slidell** (*see*) sailed on the British ship *Trent* in November, 1861, on diplomatic missions on behalf of the Confederacy. The *Trent* was stopped by an American warship, and the two Confederates were arrested. The incident nearly led to war between the United States and Britain.

Mason was released on January 1, 1862, and sailed again for England soon after. Throughout the war he worked to bring Britain into the conflict on the side of the Confederacy. After the war, fearing arrest, Mason moved to Canada, where he lived until 1868, when a Presidential proclamation of amnesty permitted him to return to Virginia.

MASON, John Y. (1799–1859). Mason was Secretary of the Navy during the Mexican War and later, while minister to France, helped to draft the **Ostend Manifesto** (*see*) in 1854. After serving (1823–1831) in the Virginia state legislature, Mason was elected to the House of Representatives. He resigned six years later in 1837 to become a federal judge. President John Tyler (1790–1862) appointed Mason Secretary of the Navy in 1844. He was the only member of Tyler's cabinet retained by President James K. Polk (1795–1849), who appointed him Attorney General (1845–1846) and then Secretary of the Navy (1846–1849). Although he was an expansionist, Mason spoke against annexing Mexico and urged the acceptance of the **Treaty of Guadalupe Hidalgo** (*see*), which ended the war. President **Franklin Pierce** (*see*) appointed Mason minister to France in 1853, a position he held until his death. At the urging of Secretary of State **William Marcy** (*see*), Mason met in Ostend, Belgium, with **James Buchanan** (*see*) and Pierre Soulé (1801–1870), the American ministers, respectively, to Britain and Spain. The three were to discuss the situation in Cuba. American slaveholders had long feared an emancipation of Cuban slaves and were anxious to acquire the island from Spain. In October, 1854, the ministers

signed a dispatch to Marcy that later became known as the Ostend Manifesto. In it, they advocated that the United States take over control of Cuba if Spain refused to sell the island. The document was later repudiated by Pierce, but Mason was allowed to remain as minister to France, a post he held until his death.

MASON AND DIXON LINE. The unofficial line between slave and free states during the Civil War, the Mason and Dixon Line divides Pennsylvania from the northern tip of Delaware, Maryland, and the part of Virginia that later became West Virginia. The boundary, which was also known as the Mason-Dixon Line, was marked out between 1763 and 1767 by two Englishmen—Charles Mason (1730–1787), an astronomer, and Jeremiah Dixon (dates unknown), a surveyor—to settle a border dispute between Maryland and Pennsylvania. The charters of the two colonies had left the border so loosely defined that Maryland's claims to Pennsylvania land even included Philadelphia, while Pennsylvania's claims included Baltimore. The line was approved by the British crown in 1769 and extended 15 years later to mark the boundary between Pennsylvania and Virginia.

MELVILLE, Herman (1819–1891). Largely ignored by literary critics during his lifetime—and for many years after his death—Melville is today recognized as one of America's greatest writers. His most important work, the novel *Moby-Dick*, is acknowledged as a classic of world literature. Melville was born in New York City. His family was poverty-stricken, and he received little formal education. He ran away to

Herman Melville

sea in 1837 and four years later became a crewman on the whaler *Acushnet*. With a friend, Melville jumped ship in the Marquesa Islands in the South Pacific and lived for a time among cannibals. Joining the crew of an Australian whaler, he visited Tahiti, Papeete, and other exotic Pacific islands. After returning to America on a navy frigate in 1844, Melville settled in Massachusetts and set about fictionalizing his experiences. Many of his accounts of adventure and romance—*Typee* (1846), *Omoo* (1847), and *Redburn* (1849)—won wide popular approval. However, his masterpiece, *Moby-Dick; or The Whale* (1851), was a commercial failure. It told the story of the relentless hunt by a captain, Ahab, for the white whale that caused the loss of his leg. "You must have plenty of sea-room to tell the truth in," Melville once explained, but the public was unable to understand the book's complex symbolism and philosophical depth. *Pierre*

(1852) also failed to attract a readership, as did *The Piazza Tales* (1856) and *The Confidence Man* (1857). Discouraged and in debt, Melville left Massachusetts and became a customs inspector in New York in 1866. His only significant literary work after that time was a long poem, *Clarel* (1876), and the short novel *Billy Budd, Foretopman,* which was not published until 1924.

N

NAT TURNER'S REBELLION. *See* **Turner, Nat.**

O

OSTEND MANIFESTO. The Ostend Manifesto—a diplomatic dispatch sent to Washington in October, 1854, by the American ministers to Britain, France, and Spain—caused a furor in the North and hostile comment abroad. Instructed by Secretary of State **William Marcy** (*see*) to shape a policy for the acquisition of Cuba, the three Americans—Pierre Soulé (1801–1870), the minister to Spain, and **James Buchanan** and **John Y. Mason** (*see both*), ministers to Britain and France, respectively—met in Ostend, Belgium, early that October. Soulé had just failed, after several months of negotiating with Spain, to purchase Cuba, but enthusiasm for territorial expansion was still strong in America. To Southerners, the possibility of annexing Cuba and establishing another slave state seemed inviting. Their fear of the emancipation of the slaves there or a revolution by the slaves on that island made such a possibility seem necessary. After conferring in Ostend, the three ministers recom-

mended in their dispatch that the United States purchase Cuba from Spain for $120,000,000. In the event Spain declined the offer, they suggested taking the island by force, saying that "then by every law, human and divine, we shall be justified in wresting it from Spain . . . ." In addition to outraging the North, the manifesto was strongly criticized in Europe, particularly in Spain. The recommendations were subsequently rejected by Marcy. Soulé, who was considered the author of it, was forced to resign.

P

"PECULIAR INSTITUTION." *See* **slavery.**

PIERCE, Franklin (1804–1869). A dark-horse candidate of the Democratic Party, Pierce won election as the 14th President of the United States in 1852 and tried vainly to reconcile Northern and Southern factions in the nation. As a result, he lost the support of his own party and was denied renomination after one term in office. Pierce was born in Hillsboro, New Hampshire. His father, Benjamin Pierce (1757–1839), was a revolutionary soldier and a governor of New Hampshire. After graduating from Bowdoin College in 1824, Pierce studied law and was admitted to the bar in 1827. Following his father into politics, Pierce was elected to the state legislature in 1829 and became its speaker in 1831. He then served in the House of Representatives (1833–1837) and the Senate (1837–1842). Pierce resigned his Senate seat to practice law in Concord, New Hampshire. He was appointed a brigadier general during the Mexican War but did not

see action. A staunch Democrat, Pierce remained active in state politics while out of office. In 1852, after the Democratic National Convention became deadlocked among **James Buchanan, Lewis Cass,** and **Stephen A. Douglas** (*see all*), Pierce was selected on the 49th ballot to run against **Winfield Scott** (*see*), the Whig Party candidate for President. Pierce was chosen because of his support of states' rights, which made him acceptable to voters in the South. He chose men from all political factions for his cabinet. However, in trying to please everyone, he satisfied no one, and his administration was a period of growing animosity between the North and the South. Inexperienced as an administrator, Pierce twice appointed inept officials to be governors of Kansas, which aggravated the turmoil in that "bleeding" territory following the **Kansas-Nebraska Act** (*see*) of 1854. Bent on territorial expansion, Pierce was instrumental in bringing about the **Gadsden Purchase** (*see*) from Mexico. Pierce's pro-Southern leanings cost him the support of Northern Democrats, and he failed to win renomination in 1856. He returned to New Hampshire, where he then fell out of favor with the voters for attacking **Abraham Lincoln** (*see*) during the Civil War. Pierce died on October 8, 1869.

POE, Edgar Allan (1809–1849). One of America's greatest poets, short-story writers, and critics, Poe created the form of the modern mystery story in such works as "The Murders in the Rue Morgue" (1841), "The Mystery of Marie Rogêt" (1842–1843), "The Gold Bug" (1843), and "The Purloined Letter" (1844). An eerie, dreamlike, and macabre world pervades all his writings. Born in

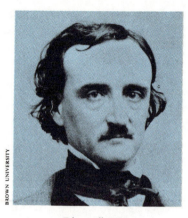

Edgar Allan Poe.

Boston, Poe was orphaned at the age of three and was brought up by John Allan (1780–1843), a prosperous Richmond merchant whose last name Poe adopted as his middle name after 1824. He studied at the University of Virginia for a term in 1826 but dropped out because of gambling debts and lack of money. The following year, he published anonymously his unsuccessful first volume, *Tamerlane and Other Poems*. After serving in the army (1827–1829), Poe published a second volume, *Al Aaraaf, Tamerlane, and Minor Poems* (1829). He entered West Point in 1830 but was expelled the following year for breaking numerous minor rules. His third volume, *Poems by Edgar A. Poe* (1831), included early versions of several poems —"To Helen," "Israfel," "The Doomed City," and "The City in the Sea." However, Poe did not gain any public recognition until 1833, when he published a short story, "A MS. Found in a Bottle." This led to his appointment as an editor on the *Southern Literary Messenger* in Richmond (1835– 1837). In 1836, Poe married his 13-year-old first cousin, Virginia Clemm (1822–1847). Two years later, he published *The Narrative*

of *Arthur Gordon Pym*. Poe then settled in Philadelphia, where he was editor, first of *Burton's Gentleman's Magazine* and then of *Graham's Magazine*. It was in this period (1838–1844) that he wrote some of his most famous short stories, including "The Masque of the Red Death" (1842), "The Tell-Tale Heart" (1843), and "The Pit and the Pendulum" (1843). In 1840, Poe published *Tales of the Grotesque and Arabesque,* which included "Ligeia" (1838) and "The Fall of the House of Usher" (1839). He became internationally famous with the publication of *The Raven and Other Poems* in 1845. After Poe's wife died in 1847, he took to drink and drugs. Nevertheless, Poe, who was always melancholy and at times mentally unbalanced, managed to produce some of his best poems. These included "Ulalume" (1847), "Eureka: A Prose Poem" (1848), "The Bells" (1849), "El Dorado" (1849), and "Annabel Lee" (1849). On September 29, 1849, Poe was in Baltimore on his way to marry a childhood sweetheart, when he disappeared. When found five days later, he was delirious. Poe died four days afterward, without having regained consciousness.

R

RHETT, Robert Barnwell (1800– 1876). An extremist newspaper publisher and Congressman from South Carolina, Rhett was known as the father of secession. Among other things, he wanted the slave trade with Africa restored. Rhett served first as a member of the House of Representatives (1837– 1849). He was appointed to fill a Senate vacancy in 1850, and at the same time he began his campaign to get South Carolina to secede

from the Union. Two years·later, disappointed that South Carolina had not seceded, Rhett resigned his seat and temporarily retired from politics. With the victory of **Abraham Lincoln** (*see*) in November, 1860, Rhett's newspaper, the Charleston *Mercury*, advocated a secession convention as soon as possible. The convention was held the following month, and on December 20, South Carolina became the first Southern state to secede. However, fellow Southerners considered Rhett too much of a firebrand to give him an important position in the Confederate government, much less the Presidency he wanted. He was elected to the Confederate Congress in 1861, but his newspaper constantly criticized the way **Jefferson Davis** (*see*) conducted the Civil War. By 1863, Rhett's own constituents had tired of him, and he was defeated for reelection. Rhett died a decade after the end of the war, still convinced the South should be separate and free.

ROEBLING, John (1806–1869). Considered the foremost American bridge builder of the 19th century, Roebling suggested and designed the Brooklyn Bridge, which his son completed. Long interested in suspension bridges, Roebling, who was born in Germany, studied civil engineering at the Royal Polytechnic Institute in Berlin. He immigrated to America in 1831, settling near Pittsburgh with a small group of German colonists. He tried farming, and after he failed, became a state engineer in 1837. Roebling subsequently worked on several state canal projects. Impressed with the frequency with which rope cables used to haul canalboats had to be replaced, Roebling conceived the idea of using wire rope in their place. In 1841, he opened a factory equipped with machinery of his own design and manufactured the first wire rope produced in America. In addition to the factory, he continued his interest in bridge construction, and in the mid-1840s built a seven-span wooden aqueduct for the Pennsylvania Canal. His first suspension bridge was constructed in 1846 over the Monongahela River at Pittsburgh. From 1848 to 1850 he built four suspension aqueducts for the Delaware and Hudson Canal. His next bridge, built in the early 1850s, was a dramatic span at Niagara Falls, connecting the New York Central Railroad with the Canadian Railway. In 1856, he began another bridge, spanning the Ohio River between Cincinnati, Ohio, and Covington, Kentucky. As early as 1857, Roebling had suggested building a bridge over New York's East River to connect Brooklyn with lower Manhattan. Ten years later, his plans were accepted, and Roebling was appointed chief engineer. While at the site of the future bridge in 1869, he was injured when a ferryboat struck a pile on which he was standing. He subsequently died of tetanus. His son, Washington Augustus Roebling (1837–1926), completed the bridge in 1883.

S

SANTA ANNA, Antonio Lopez de (1795?–1876). The commander of Mexico's army during the Mexican War, Santa Anna was forced into exile when General **Winfield Scott** (*see*) captured Mexico City on September 14, 1847. Born in Jalapa, Mexico, Santa Anna fought for Mexico's independence from Spain in 1821 and afterward, in the long, turbulent period that followed the overthrow of Spain's control, led several revolts against Mexican revolutionary leaders until he himself was elected president (1833–1835). While attempting to suppress the revolutionary movement in Texas in 1836, Santa Anna led the Mexican army that wiped out the American defenders of the Alamo on March 6, 1836 (*see pp. 562–563*). However, his forces were beaten a few weeks later at the Battle of San Jacinto, where he was captured. While a prisoner of **Sam Houston** (*see*), Santa Anna was forced to sign a secret treaty recognizing the independence of Texas, but the Mexican government later refused to abide by the pact. Although he was temporarily out of favor as a result, Santa Anna became president again in 1841. This time he ruled like a dictator and was overthrown and exiled after three years. When war with the United States appeared imminent, Santa Anna was recalled in 1846, to serve as general and later as president. Defeated at the Battles of Buena Vista and Cerro Gordo in 1847, he was forced into exile after the Americans took Mexico City. Aside from one more term as president (1853–1855), Santa Anna lived mostly in exile until 1874. He finally returned to Mexico, where he died a poor man.

SCOTT, Winfield (1786–1866). Probably the most respected American military figure in the first half of the 19th century, Scott served more than 50 years in the army and at one time ran for President. Six feet five inches tall, a stickler for detail—his men called him Old Fuss and Feathers —Scott fought in two major wars and played a key role in preventing a third. Born in Virginia, he briefly studied law before joining the army as an artillery captain in 1808. He was promoted to major general in 1814 because of his services during the War of 1812, and he took part in the Black Hawk War against the Fox and Sauk Indians in 1832. Later that year, Scott commanded the military force sent to Charleston, South Carolina, to prevent that state from repudiating federal authority during the nullification crisis. His tactful handling of the situation helped preserve peace. In 1835, he led a military campaign against the Seminole and Creek Indians in Florida, and three years afterward he supervised the relocation of the Cherokee Indians from their lands in South Carolina and Tennessee to the Southwest. In 1839, Scott negotiated a truce in the Aroostook War, a bloodless territorial dispute on the Canadian border between the United States and Britain that might have developed into an armed conflict without Scott's intervention. He was appointed general-in-chief of the army in 1841, a post he held until his retirement in 1861. Together with Generals **Zachary Taylor** and **Stephen W. Kearny** (*see both*), he played a major role in the Mexican War. After capturing the port city of Veracruz in late March, 1847 (*see pp. 572–573*), Scott continued his campaign inland, taking Mexico City on September 14, 1847 (*see pp. 548 and 578–579*). When he returned to the United States, he was acclaimed a national hero and ran as the Whig Party candidate for the Presidency in 1852, only to be defeated by **Franklin Pierce** (*see*). Scott's promotion to lieutenant general in 1852 made him the first army officer since George Washington (1732–1799) to hold that rank. At the outbreak of the Civil War in April, 1861, Scott, although a Southerner, remained loyal to the Union. He retired on November 1, 1861, because of old age.

SEWARD, William Henry (1801–1872). One of the most eloquent opponents of slavery, Seward served as Secretary of State (1861–1869) under two Presidents—**Abraham Lincoln** (*see*) and his successor, Andrew Johnson (1808–1875). Born in Florida, New York, Seward became a lawyer in 1822 and was elected governor of New York (1839–1843) before becoming a Senator (1849–1861). He opposed the **Compromise of 1850** (*see*), and on March 11, 1850, during the famous Senate debate that preceded the adoption of the various measures of the compromise, he denounced the concessions to the interests of the slave states embodied in it. Seward said there was a moral law—"a higher law than the Constitution"—that forbade any measures permitting or extending the institution of slavery. In another famous speech in 1858, Seward defined the sectional antagonism between the North and the South as "an irrepressible conflict" that would ultimately result in "either entirely a slaveholding nation or entirely a free-labor nation." President Lincoln made Seward his Secretary of State just prior to the outbreak of the Civil War in 1861. In that post, he was able to prevent European intervention in the war on the side of the South. Seward was wounded at home by assassins at the same time that Lincoln was shot on April 14, 1865, but he recovered and continued to serve as Secretary of State under President Johnson. An expansionist, Seward negotiated the purchase of Alaska from Russia in

William Henry Seward

1867—an act that was ridiculed at that time as "Seward's Folly" or "Seward's Icebox."

SLAVERY. The "peculiar institution" of the South began when the first blacks were brought from Africa to Jamestown, Virginia, in 1619. It was abolished by the passage of the Thirteenth Amendment in 1865. After the mid-17th century, when tobacco cultivation became profitable and the planta-

Caesar was the last Negro to be freed when New York State abolished slavery.

tion system required a large, cheap labor force, slavery spread from Virginia to the other colonies. The slave population rose from about 300 blacks in 1650 to more than 500,000 by 1776—or one-fifth of the total population of the 13 colonies. Although slavery was not vital on the small-scale farms of the North, New England shippers reaped huge profits by transporting natives from Africa in vessels that were notorious for their horrible conditions. Pennsylvania Quakers had denounced the evils of slavery as early as 1688, but the profitability of the slave trade often outweighed the moral arguments against it. In his first draft of the Declaration of Independence in June, 1776, Thomas Jefferson (1743–1826) condemned slavery, but Southern planters and New England merchants made him delete the statement. Beginning with Rhode Island, which abolished slavery in 1774, the New England and Middle Atlantic states gradually followed suit, and by 1846 the ownership of slaves had been abolished throughout the North. In 1787, slavery was also prohibited in the Northwest Territory, an area stretching from present-day Ohio to Wisconsin. However, in the same year, the framers of the Constitution prohibited Congress from stopping the import of slaves for 20 years after the Constitution was adopted. Meanwhile, with the invention of the cotton gin in 1793, which made possible the widespread cultivation of cotton, Southerners now needed even more slaves to work on their ever-growing plantations. As a result, the ban on the importation of slaves in 1808 was poorly enforced. Smugglers continued to bring in slaves—as many as 10,000 to 15,000 annually in the 1850s. In addition, in states such as Virginia, blacks, who were considered "chattel property," were bred and auctioned off like cattle to planters. The value of a healthy field hand between the ages of 18 and 25 jumped from about $500 in 1800 to nearly $1,800 in the late 1850s. Because the crops the planters raised—cotton, rice, and sugarcane—exhausted the soil, Southerners were eager for the United States to annex new territories (where they could continue farming) with slaves. Thus, slavery became a political issue. Sectional disputes, beginning with the admission of Missouri as a slave state in 1821, became bitter and bloody by the 1850s, when every section of national territory was divided into free and slave areas. Tension mounted with the exploits of the **underground railroad** (*see*) and the demands by abolitionists to free slaves. On the eve of the Civil War, about one-third of the nearly 12,000,000 persons living in the South were slaves.

SLIDELL, John (1793–1871). Slidell, who was a prominent Louisiana politician, was appointed United States minister to Mexico in 1845. He was asked to settle the Texas-Mexico boundary dispute —which involved the area between the Nueces River and the Rio Grande—and if possible to buy Upper California and New Mexico. However, the Mexican government refused to negotiate with him, and the United States went to war the next year to secure the territory it had hoped to acquire through diplomacy. Born in New York, Slidell moved to New Orleans in 1819, where he practiced law and was active in state politics. He served in the House of Representatives (1843–1845) and later, after his unsuccessful Mexican mission, in the Senate

(1853–1861). In February, 1861, Slidell resigned from the Senate and joined the Confederacy. He was appointed Confederate minister to France and in November, 1861, sailed for Europe along with the Confederate minister to Britain, **James M. Mason** (*see*), aboard the British vessel *Trent*. The two ministers were forcibly removed from the *Trent* by Captain Charles Wilkes (1798–1877) and taken ashore to Boston, where they were imprisoned. The *Trent* Affair, as the incident is known, almost resulted in war with Britain. However, a conflict was averted when Slidell and Mason were released and allowed to continue their journey. Slidell failed to gain French aid and recognition of the Confederacy, and he remained in Europe for the rest of his life.

SLOAT, John Drake (1781–1867). As commander of the Pacific squadron when the Mexican War broke out, Sloat occupied Monterey, California, on July 7, 1846. He hoisted the American flag and declared California annexed to the United States. Sloat was born near Goshen, New York, the son of a Revolutionary War soldier. He joined the navy as a midshipman in 1800 and a year later became a seaman on merchant ships. He was commissioned a lieutenant during the War of 1812, in which he saw limited naval duty. Until his appointment as commander in the Pacific in 1844, Sloat's naval career was fairly routine, except for two years in the mid-1820s, when, as commander of the schooner *Grampus,* he was charged with curbing piracy in the West Indies. In seizing Monterey in 1846, Sloat far exceeded his military orders, which were to occupy San Francisco and other Mexican strongholds if Mexico declared war on

the United States. On June 7, Sloat heard that Mexicans had invaded the Republic of Texas. He then immediately sailed for Monterey. Sloat received both praise and criticism for this action but was never officially reprimanded. After capturing San Francisco, Sloat, in poor health, turned over his Pacific command to Robert F. Stockton (1795–1866) on July 23. Following several years of land duty, he left the active service in 1855.

SOULÉ, Pierre. *See* **Ostend Manifesto.**

STEPHENS, Alexander Hamilton (1812–1883). A Georgia lawyer who had opposed secession, Stephens became Vice-President of the **Confederate States of America** (*see*). After serving six terms (1836–1840 and 1842) in the Georgia state legislature, Stephens was elected to the House of Representatives in 1843. Although a vigorous defender of the institution of slavery, Stephens believed that secession over the issue would be a mistake on the part of the South. He supported the **Compromise of 1850** (*see*) and campaigned in Georgia for its acceptance. Stephens retired from Congress in 1859 and returned to Georgia. In January, 1861, he voted against secession at the state convention but acquiesced when a majority favored it. On February 9, 1861, delegates to the Montgomery, Alabama, convention that set up the Confederacy selected Stephens as the Vice-President of the Confederate States. In April, **Jefferson Davis** (*see*), the President of the Confederacy, sent Stephens to Virginia to urge that state to join the rebel government. This was his last official mission for the Confederacy until February, 1865, when he headed a peace delegation that met with **Abraham Lincoln** (*see*) in Hampton Roads, Virginia. Under the Confederate constitution, Stephens' only official duty was to preside over the Senate, but he could not take part in debates. He often opposed Davis, especially after Davis suspended the writ of habeas corpus—thus imprisoning citizens without bringing charges against them—and later when Davis demanded a conscription bill. In May, 1865, federal troops arrested Stephens in Georgia, and he spent five months in a Boston prison before being freed. In 1866, he was elected to the United States Senate but was not permitted to take his seat. However, he did begin serving again in the House in 1873. He resigned that seat nine years later when he was elected governor of Georgia, the office he held at the time of his death.

STOWE, Harriet Beecher (1811–1896). Mrs. Stowe so vividly depicted the torment of slave life in her famous novel, *Uncle Tom's Cabin,* that many years later when she met **Abraham Lincoln** (*see*), the President supposedly exclaimed, "So you're the little woman who made the book that made this great war." One million copies of the book were sold before the outbreak of the Civil War, and a dramatized version played to audiences throughout the North. Mrs. Stowe was the daughter of preacher Lyman Beecher (1775–1863) and the sister of **Henry Ward Beecher** (*see*), also a noted minister. She was born in Connecticut and moved to Cincinnati in 1832, when her father was appointed president of the Lane Theological Seminary there. She married Calvin E. Stowe (1802–1886), a professor of Biblical literature, in 1836. During her 18 years in the

Midwest, Mrs. Stowe's antislavery sympathies were aroused at the seminary, a hotbed of abolitionist feeling, and at a Kentucky plantation, where she visited and saw for herself conditions under which slaves lived. In 1850, Mrs. Stowe moved to Maine, where, infuriated by the **Fugitive Slave Law** (*see*) passed that year, she began to write *Uncle Tom's Cabin, or Life Among the Lowly.* The book focuses on the adventures of Uncle Tom, a humble, devoutly Christian slave who is sold three times to various masters. He saves the life of a white girl, "little Eva," whose slave-companion is the mischievous Topsy. The villain of the book is Simon Legree, a brutal, drunken planter, who has Uncle Tom flogged to death for refusing to tell where two slaves are hiding. First published in 10 monthly installments (1851–1852) in the Washington, D.C., periodical *National Era, Uncle Tom's Cabin* came out in book form in 1852 and sold 10,000 copies within a week. Although the novel was viciously attacked by Southerners as antislavery propaganda and was criticized for factual inaccuracies, Mrs. Stowe became a worldwide celebrity. She wrote a number of other novels before

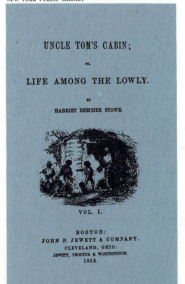

UNCLE TOM'S CABIN;

OR,

LIFE AMONG THE LOWLY.

BY

HARRIET BEECHER STOWE.

VOL. I.

BOSTON:
JOHN P. JEWETT & COMPANY.
CLEVELAND, OHIO:
JEWETT, PROCTOR & WORTHINGTON.
1852.

settling in Florida after the Civil War.

SUMNER, Charles (1811–1874). In his 23 years as a Senator (1851–1874) from Massachusetts, Sumner was an uncompromising abolitionist before the Civil War, and after it, an equally stubborn fighter for civil rights for all blacks. Born in Boston and educated at Harvard, Sumner practiced law prior to being elected to the first of his four terms in the Senate. In speeches against the Mexican War and the annexation of Texas, he became well-known as an orator. Sumner, one of the few radical abolitionists in Congress at that time, also sought the repeal of the **Fugitive Slave Law,** which was part of the **Compromise of 1850** (*see both*). In 1856, while speaking in opposition to the **Kansas-Nebraska Act** (*see*), Sumner characterized South Carolina Senator **A. P. Butler** (*see*) as a Don Quixote paying his vows to a mistress who, "though polluted in the sight of the world, is chaste in his sight. I mean the harlot, Slavery." This personal attack so angered Butler's nephew, Representative **Preston Brooks** (*see*), that two days later Brooks entered the Senate chamber and beat Sumner into unconsciousness with a cane (*see pp. 558–559*). For more than three years, Sumner was unable to return to the Senate, and he never fully recovered from the beating. Sumner became a symbol of the abolitionist cause and continued to speak in its favor when he took up his duties again. In 1861, Sumner was the first prominent statesman to advocate emancipation. Throughout the Civil War, he urged President **Abraham Lincoln** (*see*) to pay black troops on an equal basis with whites, to permit testimony by blacks in court, and to establish a Freedman's Bureau to help former slaves. As a Radical Republican after the war, Sumner agitated for an integrated public school system in the South and the right to vote by blacks. He opposed President Andrew Johnson (1808–1875) and played a large part in an attempt to impeach Lincoln's successor.

T

TAYLOR, Zachary (1784–1850). The hero of the Battle of Buena Vista during the Mexican War, Taylor became the 12th President of the United States in 1849. He died in office after 16 months and was succeeded by **Millard Fillmore** (*see*). Born in Orange County, Virginia, Taylor grew up in Kentucky and entered the United States Army in 1808 as a first lieutenant. Until 1832, when he was promoted to the rank of colonel, he served most of the time along the Southwestern and Western frontiers, fighting Indians. Taylor took part in the Black Hawk War against the Sauk and Fox Indians in 1832. He earned his nickname, Old Rough and Ready, while fighting the Seminole Indians in Florida five years later. After his victory over the Seminoles at Lake Okeechobee on December 25, 1837, Taylor was promoted to brigadier general and served (1838–1840) as commander of the Department of Florida. In the summer of 1845, President James Polk (1795–1849) ordered Taylor to Texas to protect the border from expected Mexican attacks. The area between the Nueces River and Rio Grande was then claimed by both Texas and Mexico. Taylor reached Corpus Christi on the Nueces in July and the following January was ordered to advance to the Rio Grande. He arrived at the river's northern bank opposite the Mexican town of Matamoros in late March. On April 25, some of his men were ambushed by Mexican troops. Then, less than a week before the United States officially declared war on Mexico on May 13, 1846, Taylor defeated Mexican forces on two successive days at the Battles of Palo Alto and Resaca de la Palma. Taylor was subsequently named commander of the army of the Rio Grande, and crossing that river, he seized control of Matamoros on May 18 and later captured the stronghold of Monterrey on September 24. Taylor then made a truce with the Mexicans, but Polk refused to approve it and ordered him to press the war. Finally, in one of the most significant actions of the Mexican War, Taylor advanced from Monterrey to Buena Vista early in 1847, where he defeated the Mexican general **Santa Anna** (*see*), thus ending the fighting in northern Mexico. This victory gained Taylor the Whig Party nomination for the Presidency in the election of 1848, which he won over his Democratic opponent, **Lewis Cass** (*see*). The main issue of Taylor's administration was whether slavery should be prohibited or allowed in the territory acquired from Mexico by the **Treaty of Guadalupe Hidalgo** (*see*). Although he had not spelled out his political ideals during the campaign, Taylor, a Southerner by birth, emerged after his inauguration as a firm supporter of national unity rather than sectionalist policies. He opposed the admission of Texas into the Union as a slave state and urged that California be admitted as a free state. Similarly, Taylor hoped that the territories of Utah and New Mexico would be organized with-

Zachary Taylor

out permitting slavery. Taylor suffered a stomach ailment after a Fourth of July ceremony in Washington, D.C., and died five days later. The question of slavery in the new territories was settled later that summer by the **Compromise of 1850** (*see*).

TOOMBS, Robert Augustus (1810–1885). Born in Georgia, Toombs was a longtime moderate who became an ardent secessionist and later served the Confederacy as Secretary of State and brigadier general. He was elected to the House of Representatives (1845–1853) and later to the Senate (1853–1861). Toombs supported the **Compromise of 1850** (*see*) and campaigned in Georgia for its acceptance. Dismayed by the election of **Abraham Lincoln** (*see*), he nevertheless backed the **Crittenden Compromise** (*see*), hoping to preserve the Union. When it failed, Toombs urged Georgia's immediate secession. Toombs was disappointed when he was chosen Secretary of State and not President of the **Confederate States of America** (*see*). Boredom and differences with **Jefferson Davis** (*see*) led to his resignation five months later. Commissioned a brigadier general, Toombs demanded a promotion after the Battle of Antietam on September 17, 1862. He resigned when this was refused and continued his criticism of Davis as a private citizen. In 1865, Toombs fled to England to avoid capture by Union troops. Two years later, he returned to America and took a prominent part in Georgia politics, although he would not take an oath of allegiance to the United States.

TRAVIS, William Barret (1809–1836). "The Gallant Travis," as his friends called him, shared command of the Texas forces at the Alamo with **James Bowie** (*see*). One of the youngest leaders in the Texas revolution against Mexico, Travis, a native of South Carolina, began practicing law in Alabama before he was 20. In 1831, he moved to Texas. There he became interested in local politics, aligning himself with settlers who were ready to defend their rights forcibly against the Mexicans. When General **Santa Anna** (*see*) sent soldiers to regarrison the abandoned fort at Anahuac in 1835, Travis formed a group of volunteers and captured the Mexicans. During the American siege of San Antonio later the same year, he took command of a scouting company. At the close of 1835, Travis was ordered to reinforce the Alamo. Arriving there in February, 1836, with 25 men, he and Bowie were given joint command of the 186 men at the mission-fort. On February 24, the day after Santa Anna's army reached the Alamo, Bowie fell ill, leaving the 27-year-old Travis in sole command. Ordered by Santa Anna to surrender, Travis answered by having a cannon fired into the

William Barret Travis

enemy lines. He and all the defenders, Bowie included, were slain after a gallant defense on March 6, 1836, when the Alamo fell.

TREATY OF GUADALUPE HIDALGO. Signed February 2, 1848, in Guadalupe Hidalgo, a village outside of Mexico City, this treaty officially ended the Mexican War and added more than 500,000 square miles of territory to the United States. The territory included all or parts of the present-day states of Arizona, California, Colorado, New Mexico, Texas, Utah, and Wyoming. Early in 1847, President James K. Polk (1795–1849) sent **Nicholas Trist** (*see*) to Mexico, authorizing him to negotiate a peace. The mission might never have led to a treaty, because Polk soon grew to distrust Trist. One reason was Trist's friendship with Polk's political rival, General **Winfield Scott** (*see*). Another was the long time that Trist was taking to con-

duct negotiations with the Mexican general **Santa Anna** (*see*). Angered at the way things were going, Polk ordered Trist to return to Washington in November, 1847. However, Trist, who thought peace would be impossible to achieve unless reached then, disobeyed Polk's orders. He remained in Mexico and finally signed a treaty with a new government in 1848. The treaty fulfilled all of Polk's original instructions. Mexico recognized the Rio Grande as the Texas boundary and ceded the territories of New Mexico and California. The United States agreed to pay Mexico $15,000,000 and to assume the more than $3,000,000 in debts that Mexico owed to American citizens. The sum paid to Mexico was about $10,000,000 less than the amount **John Slidell** (*see*) had been instructed to offer for the same territories just before the war broke out in 1846. Although Trist was dismissed when he returned home, Polk recommended to Congress that it ratify the treaty he had signed. It went into effect on July 4, 1848.

TRIST, Nicholas (1800–1874). As a special envoy of the State Department, Trist negotiated the **Treaty of Guadalupe Hidalgo** (*see*), which ended the Mexican War. The Virginia-born diplomat cemented his political connections by marrying a granddaughter of Thomas Jefferson (1743–1826). Trist served briefly in 1829 as private secretary to Andrew Jackson (1767–1845) and in 1833 was appointed consul to Havana. There, he was accused of failing to protect American citizens, fawning to the Spanish, and fostering the slave trade. The charges were never proved, but Trist was removed from his post in 1841.

Under President James K. Polk (1795–1849), Trist became chief clerk of the State Department, and in early 1847 he was chosen to conclude a peace treaty with the Mexican government. Upon his arrival in Mexico, Trist tried to reach a quick settlement in order to prevent anarchy in Mexico, but Polk began to demand severer peace terms. When Trist agreed to a boundary not listed in his instructions, he was recalled in November, 1847. Disobeying the order, Trist remained in Mexico and on February 2, 1848, signed the Treaty of Guadalupe Hidalgo, according to the terms of his original instructions. Although the United States accepted the treaty, it refused to compensate Trist immediately for his efforts. He later had an unsuccessful law practice.

TRUMBULL, Lyman (1813–1896). Trumbull, an early friend and supporter of **Abraham Lincoln** (*see*), was an Illinois Senator who introduced the resolution that became the basis for the Thirteenth Amendment, which outlawed slavery. A lawyer, Trumbull served as a justice of the Illinois supreme court from 1848 to 1853. In 1854, he was elected to the House of Representatives but never took his seat because he was appointed to the Senate before Congress met, to fill out an unexpired term. Although Trumbull was a Democrat, Lincoln supported him when he ran for a full term in the Senate that same year because Trumbull favored granting free land to the homesteaders. Trumbull was elected, and before secession became imminent, he switched allegiance to the Republican Party. During the Civil War, Trumbull began attacking Lincoln for the suspension of certain constitutional rights, such as the writ of habeas corpus. He introduced in 1864 the resolution on which the Thirteenth Amendment is based. During the Reconstruction Era, Trumbull voted with the Radical Republicans, but he refused to do so when Congress tried to impeach President Andrew Johnson (1808–1875) in 1868. One of only seven Republicans who did not vote for impeachment, Trumbull lost the support of his party and was never again elected to the Senate. He returned to the Democratic Party and ran unsuccessfully for governor of Illinois.

TRUTH, Sojourner (1797?–1883?). One of the most eloquent abolitionist orators was an illiterate woman who was born a slave in upstate New York. The tall, gaunt black woman, originally named Isabella, had 13 children, most of whom were sold to slave owners. She was freed in 1827 under the state's policy of gradual emancipation, and after a few years of freedom, became fired with religious zeal to help her people. She changed her name to Sojourner Truth and dedicated herself to freeing all slaves in the nation. Sojourner left New York in 1843 with only a bag of clothes and 25¢ and began crusading at antislavery meetings throughout the North. The stories she told of black suffering were so moving that she won many converts to the abolitionist cause. Sojourner also became an advocate of women's rights, and later in life she waged battles against racial segregation. She was so adamant in refusing to sit in the black section of streetcars in Washington D.C., that the conductors left her alone.

TUBMAN, Harriet (1821?–1913). This fugitive slave who became a renowned abolitionist and agent on the **underground railroad** (*see*), was referred to as The Moses of Her People because she led more than 300 slaves to freedom in the North and Canada. Harriet was born a slave in Maryland. From the time that she was put to work at the age of six, she was insubordinate to her overseers, was frequently punished, and was once hit so hard on the head that she suffered from dizzy spells the rest of her life. She finally made her break for freedom about 1849, and after being shuttled from station to station on the underground railroad, she reached Philadelphia. Harriet herself subsequently became a dauntless, shrewd member of the escape network. She often risked capture and execution—at one point, rewards for her arrest totaled more than $40,000—and

Harriet Tubman

even brought her parents out of the South in 1857. During such hazardous operations, she would threaten the escaped slaves with death if they spoke of surrendering or returning to bondage. Once, while in Canada, Harriet met **John Brown** (*see*), who called her General Tubman and enlisted her aid in liberating slaves in Virginia. During the Civil War, Harriet first worked as a nurse for the Union Army in South Carolina. In 1863, she went to Georgia and Florida as a Union spy and guided all-black Union regiments on their raids in those states. Emerging from the war a heroine, Harriet worked to secure civil rights for freedmen. She settled in Auburn, New York, and used the proceeds from a biography, first published in 1869 by her friends, to found a charitable institution for poor blacks known as the Harriet Tubman Home.

This engraving from an 1861 antislavery book depicts the capture of Nat Turner.

TURNER, Nat (1800–1831). The leader of a sensational slave rebellion at Southampton, Virginia, in August of 1831, Turner showed an aptitude for learning as a young boy. One of his master's sons taught him to read, and he soon became familiar with the Bible. Believing himself divinely destined to deliver his people from slavery, he became a lay preacher and a leader among the blacks in his neighborhood. Turner interpreted an eclipse of the sun in February, 1831, as a sign of divine approval to revolt against his master. On August 21, he and seven other slaves killed the six members of the Travis family, who had acquired Turner the previous year. Obtaining weapons and horses from farms in the neighborhood, he enlisted about 50 additional slaves in the revolt. By the following evening, they had killed more than 50 white persons. The slave owners then organized a massive manhunt, during which about 100 blacks were killed. Turner went into hiding near the Travis farm but was captured on October 30. On November 11, he was hanged with about 20 of his followers. The widespread terror created by the rebellion led to a tightening of restrictions on slaves. William Styron's controversial *The Confessions of Nat Turner,* published in 1967, is based on a confession Turner made before his execution.

U

UNCLE TOM'S CABIN. *See* **Stowe, Harriet Beecher.**

UNDERGROUND RAILROAD. The underground railroad was a secret and loose-knit network of abolitionists who, in the 1840s and 1850s, helped escaped slaves flee to free states in the North and Canada. The term *underground railroad* was said to have originated when a Southerner, in pursuit of his missing slave, lost track of him at Ripley, Ohio, and exclaimed that he must have used an "underground road" to escape. The escape route was staffed by about 3,000 "conductors," including religious groups, free blacks in the North, and noted abolitionists such as **John Brown**. Working mainly at night, the conductors devised hiding places for the runaways and used ingenious disguises to spirit their passengers from place to place. At each station, they received asylum and money. The escape network eventually covered 14 Northern states from Maine to Nebraska, with complex systems of routes running from west to east and from north to south. Stowaways from South-

Slaves escaped to freedom with the help of farmers along the underground railroad.

ern ports came to New England and then were shipped to Nova Scotia and New Brunswick, Canada, or sometimes England. Others, congregating at towns along the Great Lakes, entered Canada by way of Ontario. According to one estimate, about 75,000 of the nearly 4,000,000 slaves in the South escaped to freedom via the underground in the two decades preceding the Civil War.

WALKER, James (1819–1889). This English-born artist specialized in painting historical scenes. When a child, Walker migrated to New York City with his parents. He later moved to Mexico City and was there at the outbreak of the Mexican War in 1846. Fleeing the Mexican capital, he joined the American army as an interpreter and was present when the Americans seized and occupied Mexico City in 1847. Walker later

painted a mural of the Battle of Chapultepec Hill, on the outskirts of the city, for the Capitol in Washington, D.C. (*see pp. 576–577*). He also painted 12 other scenes from the Mexican War for the United States War Department building. Later, Walker painted battle scenes from the Civil War.

WEBSTER, Daniel (1782–1852). Known as the Defender of the Constitution, Webster was one of the leading American statesmen of the 19th century (*see pp. 620–628*). Only Henry Clay (1777–1852) and John C. Calhoun (1782–1850) rivaled him for dominance in Congress in the decades preceding the Civil War. Webster never attained his ambition to be President. His alliance with conservative business interests deprived him of a large popular base, and his belief that the Union should be preserved at all costs—which led him to support such measures as the **Compromise**

of 1850 (*see*)—diminished his support in both the North and the South. Webster was born in New Hampshire. He graduated from Dartmouth College in 1801 and became a lawyer in Boston (1805–1807) and then in Portsmouth, New Hampshire (1807–1816). He was a Representative from New Hampshire (1813–1817) before moving back to Boston in 1816. He represented Massachusetts in the House (1823–1827) and in the Senate (1827–1841 and 1845–1850). Webster's brilliance as a constitutional lawyer before the Supreme Court, especially in the Dartmouth College case of 1819 (*see p. 371*), gained him national prominence. His thundering speeches in the Senate, in which he championed federalism against such advocates of states' rights as Robert Y. Hayne (1791–1839) in 1830 and Calhoun in 1833, spread his fame. Together with Clay, Webster led the Whig Party and in 1836 was the unsuccessful Presidential candidate of the New England faction of the Whigs. As Secretary of State (1841–1843) under John Tyler (1790–1862), he negotiated the Webster-Ashburton Treaty with Britain, which fixed the present border with Canada in the Northeast. Webster again headed the State Department (1850–1852) under **Millard Fillmore** (*see*). Webster's death, shortly after his retirement in 1852, was an occasion of national mourning.

WEED, Thurlow (1797–1882). A powerful political boss in the Whig Party, and after 1854, in the Republican Party, Weed is credited with securing the Presidential nominations of William Henry Harrison (1773–1841) in 1836 and 1840, Henry Clay (1777–1852) in 1844, **Zachary Taylor**

(*see*) in 1848, and **Winfield Scott** (*see*) in 1852. Of the four men, Harrison and Taylor were elected President. Weed was born in Greene County, New York. His family was poor, and as a youth he was apprenticed to a printer in Onondaga, New York. For a number of years he worked at various newspaper jobs in central New York, acquiring a considerable knowledge of local political affairs. He became editor of the Albany *Evening Journal* in 1830, a post he held until 1862. Essentially a political manipulator and "vote-getter," Weed was little concerned with issues or principles. Although never accused of taking graft himself, he considered bribery and the "spoils system" as necessary ingredients for political success. Weed was first successful when he brought about the election of his lifelong friend, **William H. Seward** (*see*), as governor of New York in 1838. Twenty-two years later, when he failed to get the Republican Presidential nomination for Seward, he supported **Abraham Lincoln** (*see*). Lincoln then sent him on an unofficial diplomatic mission to Britain in 1861. Poor health forced Weed into semiretirement in the late 1860s.

WELLES, Gideon (1802–1878). Welles, who helped found the Republican Party in 1854, was Secretary of the Navy during the Civil War. A native of Connecticut, Welles studied law but decided to become a journalist. In 1826, he became editor and co-owner of the Hartford *Times*. He also was elected to the state legislature (1827–1835) at this time and advocated reform causes and the policies of President Andrew Jackson (1767–1845). Jackson came to rely on Welles for

advice and named him postmaster (1836–1841) of Hartford. Welles eventually quit the Democratic Party over the slavery issue. He aided in organizing the Republicans, and in 1856 he established the Hartford *Evening Press,* a Republican organ in which Welles emerged as one of the leading political writers who advocated moderation. Upon becoming President, **Abraham Lincoln** (*see*) appointed Welles Secretary of the Navy (1861–1869). He speedily overhauled the Union's naval forces, which at the beginning of the Civil War were outmoded. Welles is credited with masterminding brilliant naval attacks, the successful blockading of Southern ports, and encouraging the building of ironclad ships— all important factors in defeating the Confederacy.

WHIPPER, William (dates unknown). Whipper—the son of a white father and a free Negro— was a successful businessman who took part in the abolitionist movement in the first half of the 19th century. Born in Pennsylvania, Whipper educated himself and eventually inherited his father's lumber business. About 1835, he helped to found a Negro abolitionist group, the American Moral Reform Society. The society promoted Negro education, a Negro press, and histories of the Negro people. Whipper advocated integrated schools and churches. In an 1837 newspaper editorial, he suggested that passive resistance be used to attain Negro goals. It is thought that Whipper lived until the 1880s.

WILMOT, David (1814–1868). By trying to attach a rider to a bill appropriating funds for peace negotiations with Mexico in 1846,

Wilmot, an otherwise little-known Democratic Representative from Pennsylvania, made his name famous. The **Wilmot Proviso** (*see*), which would have barred slavery in any territory acquired as a result of the Mexican War, was not adopted by Congress, but its ban on slavery in new territories became the platform of moderate abolitionists. Wilmot, a lawyer and one of the founders of the Republican Party, entered the House in 1845 and served in it until 1851, when he was appointed chief judge of the 13th judicial district of Pennsylvania. After remaining on the bench for 10 years, he was elected Senator (1861–1863). He resigned to serve, until his death, as a judge on the United States Court of Claims.

WILMOT PROVISO. The sectional controversy raging over slavery in America was further inflamed on August 8, 1846, when **David Wilmot** (*see*), a Democratic Congressman from Pennsylvania, tried to attach a rider to a bill being considered by Congress. The bill was a request by President James K. Polk (1795–1849) for $2,000,000 to use in negotiating peace with Mexico. The Wilmot Proviso stipulated that "neither slavery nor involuntary servitude" would ever exist in any territory acquired from Mexico with the funds. The proviso was supported by those morally opposed to slavery, by others who feared that Southern power would increase with the extension of slavery in new states, and by opponents of Polk. The amended bill was adopted in the House in 1846 but not acted upon by the Senate before its adjournment that year. In 1847, a bill for a $3,000,000 appropriation was introduced in the House, amended as before by

Wilmot, and passed. The Senate, however, refused to vote on the amended bill and passed its own bill for the same amount without Wilmot's rider. After bitter debate, the House finally accepted the Senate version. The Wilmot Proviso, though defeated, provoked heated debates over slavery in both the North and the South. Its principle of prohibiting slavery in newly acquired territory became a major rallying point that eventually led to the founding of the Republican Party in 1854. The issue was a crucial plank in the platform on which **Abraham Lincoln** (*see*) was elected President in 1860.

WOOL, John Ellis (1784–1869). This career army officer is best remembered for his distinguished service in the Mexican War. Born in Newburgh, New York, Wool received little education. He was commissioned a captain at the outbreak of the War of 1812, and within four years he had risen to colonel and inspector general of the army, a rank he retained until 1841, when he was promoted to brigadier general. At the start of the Mexican War in 1846, Wool went to Cincinnati, where he recruited about 12,000 volunteers in six weeks. He then went to San Antonio to prepare for an expedition through northern Mexico. Leading a force of 1,400 soldiers, and training and disciplining them along the way, Wool marched across 900 miles of rough, hostile terrain in almost three months' time without any serious mishaps and arrived at Saltillo, in northeastern Mexico, in December, 1846. At the ensuing Battle of Buena Vista, Wool was second in command to **Zachary Taylor** (*see*). He displayed such skill and fortitude during the battle that Con-

gress later awarded him a sword and a citation. After the war, Wool held several high military commands until his retirement in 1863.

Y

YANCEY, William Lowndes (1814–1863). One of the foremost leaders in the secessionist movement, Yancey was instrumental in the formation of the **Confederate States of America** (*see*) in 1860. He was the author of the so-called Alabama platform, which became the credo of the South. Yancey was born in Georgia. He attended Williams College in Massachusetts from 1830 to 1833 and afterward became a lawyer in Alabama. After serving in the Alabama legislature (1841–1844), Yancey was elected to the House of Representatives in 1844. He was reelected in 1846 but resigned almost immediately out of disgust for Northern Democrats, who failed to support his proslavery views. Two years later, Yancey drafted the Alabama platform. It emphasized

the doctrine of states' rights and declared that it was the duty of Congress to protect property—meaning slaves, which Southerners considered property. From 1848 to 1861, Yancey continually urged Southerners to forget about compromise within existing political parties. He advocated that they form a new party based on common sectional interests. During the campaign of 1860, Yancey proposed that the South secede from the Union if a Republican was elected President. When a revised version of his Alabama platform was not adopted at the Democratic National Convention, Yancey and a majority of Southern delegates stormed out and subsequently formed the Constitutional Democratic Party, which nominated **John C. Breckinridge** (*see*) for President. After Lincoln's victory, Yancey drew up Alabama's ordinance of secession. He served briefly as the Confederate commissioner to Britain and France, and when he returned from abroad in 1862, he represented Alabama in the Confederate Senate until his death.

Yancey's call for secession was echoed at rallies held throughout the South.